Nothing and Everything

SILVIA KOLBOWSKI

Rien et tout

Commissaire / Curator
Michèle Thériault

Galerie Leonard & Bina Ellen Art Gallery
Université Concordia University

I would like to thank Silvia Kolbowski for closely collaborating on this exhibition project and on the discussion published in this catalogue. I greatly appreciate the acuteness of her thought, her critical engagement with her art practice and, of course, the long hours spent crafting her commentaries. I would also like to thank Rosalind Deutsche and Christopher Bedford who granted permission for the reprinting of their essays. Emmelyne Pornillos developed a graphic concept for this publication with her usual sensitivity. My appreciation for the Gallery staff is renewed with each exhibition. **M.T.**

Je remercie Silvia Kolbowski pour sa collaboration entière à ce projet d'exposition et d'échange. J'ai fort apprécié l'acuité de sa pensée, son regard critique sur sa pratique artistique et, bien sûr, les longues heures passées à façonner ses commentaires. Je remercie aussi Rosalind Deutsche et Christopher Bedford d'avoir permis la reproduction de leurs essais. Emmelyne Pornillos a conçu le graphisme de cet ouvrage avec sa sensibilité habituelle. Mon appréciation du personnel de la Galerie est renouvellée à chaque exposition. **M.T.**

PREFACE / PRÉFACE 2
Michèle Thériault

AN INADEQUATE HISTORY OF CONCEPTUAL ART 7
Silvia Kolbowski

NARRATIVES / RÉCITS
Male Voice 14 / Female Voice 18

INADEQUACY / INADÉQUATION 21
Rosalyn Deutsche

MODELS OF INTERVENTION: A DISCUSSION BETWEEN
MICHÈLE THÉRIAULT AND SILVIA KOLBOWSKI 41

AFTER HIROSHIMA MON AMOUR 69
Silvia Kolbowski

AFTER AND BEFORE / APRÈS ET AVANT 72
Christopher Bedford

WORKS EXHIBITED / ŒUVRES EXPOSÉES 85

PREFACE

Incisive, engaged, and particularly rich in meaning, Silvia Kolbowski's work constitutes itself as an object and a field of resistance. In conversation with artist Walid Raad, Kolbowski states that she can only evolve as an artist within a culture of political resistance. But what form does an artist's contribution take in such a context?

> [...] I think that artists can contribute by using images, words, sounds, the body, and objects in ways that do not instrumentalize power and commerce, by making work that offers a spectatorial position that foregrounds the structures of the unconscious in relation to the political realm, and maintains a social and historical space for experiencing those structures in a world that favours an eternal present.[1]

This is a particularly demanding program for an artist to follow. The instrumentalization of power and commerce has infiltrated all spheres of life, manifesting itself in the most unexpected ways, so that one might unintentionally acquiesce to its processes, and sustain them. And the art milieu is a particularly insidious example of this. Arresting this process requires vigilance, insight, strategy, and critical thinking. Kolbowski has practiced this vigilance with acuity throughout her career, beginning in the late 1970s in New York, through photographic works, public interventions, and site specific installations that have examined, on different levels and with a particular sensitivity to the socio-political climate in which her practice evolved, what is at stake in representation. Feminism and psychoanalytic theory have been essential in the elaboration of her work, and it is these modes of thought and analysis, together with an ethical questioning of the vocabulary of art and of the artist, that have enabled her to *actualize* resistance in her work.

This exhibition presents two major works, produced ten years apart, which consider very different contemporary issues. On the one hand, *an inadequate history of conceptual art* (1998–1999) reflects upon the renewed interest in Conceptual Art, and on the other, *After Hiroshima Mon Amour* (2008), engages with American military interventions in Iraq and the associated criminal neglect. These works offer subtle and provocative explorations of the meeting of unconscious forces with social, political, and historical structures as they are imbricated, not only with these events, but also with forms of art, cinema and writing that have radically transformed existing conventions. The rich and complex works presented in this exhibition reveal the artist's thought processes and underline the significance of her work.

Michèle Thériault, Director

1 *Between Artists: Silvia Kolbowski in conversation with Walid Raad* (New York: A.R.T. Press, 2006), 70–71.

PRÉFACE

Incisive, engagée et particulièrement riche de sens, l'œuvre de Silvia
Kolbowski se constitue en objet et en champ de résistance. Dans un dialogue
avec l'artiste Walid Raad, Kolbowski affirme ne pouvoir évoluer en tant
qu'artiste que dans le cadre d'une culture de résistance politique. Mais à quoi
peut ressembler la contribution d'un artiste dans un tel contexte ?

> [...] je crois que les artistes peuvent contribuer en utilisant des images, des mots,
> des sons, le corps de manière à ne pas instrumentaliser le pouvoir et le commerce,
> en créant des œuvres qui offrent une position de spectateur où sont mises en
> relief les structures de l'inconscient en rapport avec le domaine politique, et dans
> laquelle perdure un espace social et historique permettant d'expérimenter ces
> structures au sein d'un monde favorisant un présent éternel[1].

Il est particulièrement difficile pour une artiste de suivre ce chemin exigeant,
car l'instrumentalisation du pouvoir et du commerce s'immisce dans toutes les
sphères de la vie, se manifestant de manières inattendues, de telle sorte qu'on
y acquiesce et la nourrit à notre insu. Et le milieu de l'art en est une incidence
particulièrement insidieuse. La mettre en échec est affaire de vigilance, de savoir,
de stratégie et d'analyse critique. Silvia Kolbowski a su exercer cette vigilance
avec acuité, tout au long d'une carrière débutée à la fin des années soixante-dix
à New York, dans des œuvres photographiques, des interventions publiques et
des installations ciblées qui ont interrogé sur différents registres les enjeux de la
représentation avec une sensibilité toute particulière pour le climat sociopolitique
dans lequel sa pratique évoluait. Le féminisme et la théorie psychanalytique ont
été déterminants dans l'élaboration de son œuvre, et ce sont ces modes de
pensée et d'analyse unis à un questionnement éthique quant au vocabulaire de
l'art et de l'artiste, qui lui permirent de *faire* résistance avec son œuvre.

Cette exposition présente deux œuvres majeures réalisées à dix ans
d'intervalle qui réfléchissent sur des questions d'actualité très différentes.
D'une part, sur la résurgence de l'art conceptuel (*an inadequate history of
conceptual art,* 1998–1999), et d'autre part, sur les incursions militaires
américaines en Iraq et la négligence criminelle qui en découle (*After Hiroshima
Mon Amour,* 2008). Elles explorent subtilement et avec provocation la rencontre
des voies de l'inconscient avec les structures sociales, politiques et historiques
dans leur imbrication non seulement avec ces situations, mais aussi avec des
manières de faire et de penser l'art, l'écriture et le cinéma qui ont bouleversé les
formes établies. Ces œuvres, riches et complexes, font mieux connaître au
visiteur les mécanismes de la pensée de Kolbowski et lui permettront de bien
saisir la portée de ce travail.

Michèle Thériault, directrice

---

1   *Between Artists: Silvia Kolbowski in conversation with
    Walid Raad* (New York: A.R.T. Press, 2006), p. 70–71.

an inadequate history of conceptual art (1998–1999)

Silvia Kolbowski

After a number of years of observing the resurgent interest in Conceptual art in Europe, the United States, and parts of Asia and Latin America, I was motivated to produce a project that would raise some questions about its return. This return has taken various forms: retrospectives, revived careers, academic and press attention, market interest, the coining of the term neo-conceptualism, and, more recently, books. The intended purpose of this project was to slow down the rapidity with which this return occurred, in order to be able to look more closely at its significance. I thought that if I asked artists to speak from memory about conceptual projects from the past, the recountings would include both valuable recollections and the fallacies of human memory. It seemed that these fallacies, the stutters of memory, so to speak, could trouble the fluidity of the official return.

In 1998, I sent letters to sixty artists, asking them to participate in this project. Forty artists agreed to respond to the following statement: "Briefly describe a conceptual art work, not your own, of the period between 1965 and 1975, which you personally witnessed/experienced at the time. For the sake of this project, the definition of conceptual art would be broad enough to encompass such phenomena of that period as actions documented through drawings, photographs, films, and video; concepts executed in the form of drawings or photographs; objects where the end product is primarily a record of the precipitant concept, and performative activities which sought to question the conventions of dance and theater."

The artists were told not mention their own names, the names of the artists whose work they described, or the titles of the works. They *could* mention the dates of the works and the locations. In addition, their hands were videotaped in close-up while their accounts were being audio-recorded. In the resultant audio-video installation, the large projected images of their hands play *without sound and out of synch* with the audio component of the artists' voices.

Another version of this text was published in *October* 92 (Spring 2000).

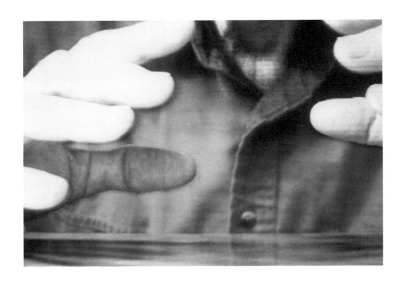

an inadequate history of conceptual art (1998–1999)

Silvia Kolbowski

Après quelques années à observer l'intérêt renouvelé envers l'art conceptuel en Europe, aux États-Unis et dans différentes parties de l'Asie et de l'Amérique latine, j'ai voulu réaliser un projet qui soulèverait certaines questions à propos de sa résurgence. Celle-ci a revêtu diverses formes : rétrospectives, carrières relancées, attention universitaire et médiatique, engouement commercial, création du terme néo-conceptualisme, et, plus récemment, production d'ouvrages. L'objectif de mon projet était de freiner la rapidité de ce retour, afin de pouvoir mieux analyser sa signification. J'ai pensé qu'en demandant à des artistes de faire appel à leur mémoire au sujet de projets conceptuels du passé, que leurs récits jumelleraient la pertinence d'un témoignage avec les erreurs de la mémoire humaine. Il m'a semblé que ces erreurs, les bégaiements de la mémoire, pour ainsi dire, pouvaient troubler la fluidité de la résurgence officielle.

En 1998, j'ai écrit à soixante artistes, leur demandant de participer à ce projet. Quarante d'entre eux ont accepté de réagir à l'énoncé suivant : « Décrivez brièvement une œuvre d'art conceptuel, créée par une autre personne que vous au cours de la période allant de 1965 à 1975, dont vous avez personnellement fait l'expérience ou avez été témoin à l'époque. Aux fins de ce projet, la définition d'art conceptuel doit être suffisamment large pour inclure des phénomènes de cette époque, tels que des actions documentées par des dessins, des photographies, des films et des vidéos ; des concepts matérialisés sous forme de dessins ou de photographies ; des objets où le produit est avant tout la retombée documentaire d'un concept afférent, ainsi que des activités de performance qui visaient à remettre en question les formes établies de la danse et du théâtre ».

On demanda aux artistes de ne pas mentionner leurs noms, le nom des artistes qui avaient réalisé l'œuvre qu'ils décrivaient, ou le titre de celle-ci. Ils *pouvaient* mentionner la date de réalisation de l'œuvre et son lieu de présentation. En outre, leurs mains étaient captées en gros plan tandis que leurs témoignages étaient enregistrés. Il en est résulté une installation vidéo et audio dans laquelle les images projetées grand format de leurs mains sont présentées *sans le son et de manière désynchronisée* par rapport à l'élément audio comportant les voix des artistes.

Une autre version de ce texte est parue dans *October* 92 (printemps 2000).

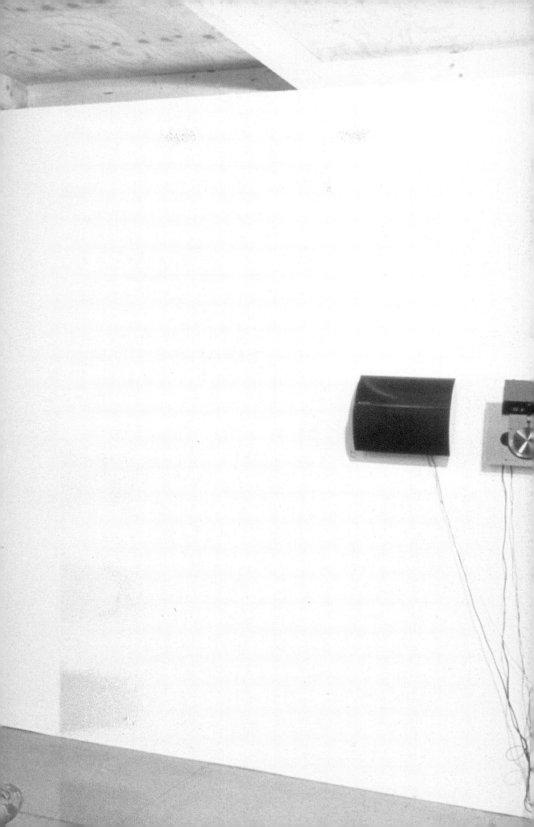

MALE VOICE

Let me think. Right. The piece I'm going to talk about was, let's see, it must have been early or mid-seventies. It was a performance at 112 Greene St. And it was in the evening. This was when 112 was real funky, and I remember seeing a lot of green paint crumbling off the walls. This was a performance that took place in the elevator shaft. The artist was in the elevator shaft, and he was going to invite three people to come into the elevator shaft and to stick pins in him.

I found that a very strange thing, but I think what was strange was that there were quite a lot of people – I can't remember how many, maybe 50 or 60 people. And I think what struck me about the whole thing was the audience's response. 'Cause the elevator shaft looked, it had that greeney kind of paint that old lofts had, and a little kind of window, I remember seeing a kind of – I never actually saw the person in there. Maybe I did, I think I saw him lying down, with just his pants on, lying on some kind of table or something. Through the window. And there was a kind of guard at the door saying we weren't allowed in, we could look through. It looked a little bit like a kind of execution chamber. I thought this is a very strange kind of thing to look at.

But the people there were sort of festive; it struck me as a little bit like a carnival. I mean people had wine and they were standing around and talking about when's it going to happen, and whose going to go in there and do this, and people would joke and say well what if they stick the pins in his eyes, or they stick him in his testicles – I mean where are they going to stick these pins, who's going to do it? (laughter) And I can't remember exactly what was going on, but it seemed like we were there for like an hour, and people were starting to get really impatient. I could see that people were starting to get really pissed off that they had to stand there and hang around. It wasn't getting unruly, but it was a little bit like a carnival show. I was thinking, I mean what am I doing here? Why do I need to look at this, to see someone get stabbed with pins?

And then someone said, ok we're going to start, and everyone really wanted to be selected to go in and do this. And then all of a sudden they open up the door and I remember people saying "his friends are here, his friends are here." And then people said it's a setup, he's only going to have some friends come in, so they'll stick him in his fingers or something, they're not going to stick him in his eyes. I mean (laughter) it was really a very strange response, and then the door opened and somebody went in and came out, and then somebody else went in and did it, and nobody ever saw where the pins were stuck or how they were stuck. And that was it! It was very anticlimactic, in the sense that there was no drama. But I guess the reason that I'm talking about it is that it stuck with me for a long time as to what this was all about. And I guess the question was what it wasn't about. I think the reason that it stuck with me so long was that it wasn't about a sort of aestheticization of objects, I guess it was about tension, the psychological space of people being invited to penetrate this person's body, the danger of it, the temporariness of it, and it could, I guess, have been really nasty. But it worked out kind of fine I guess.

But the whole thing still has a kind of resonance with me, in terms of why people ... as a piece of sculpture, the idea of stabbing someone with little pins. I still think it was kind of powerful. Today, imagine someone doing that – it could be deadly, you'd think there could be AIDS, there'd be all kinds of contamination. The risk factor would probably increase a lot.

VOIX D'HOMME

Laissez-moi y penser. Bon. La pièce dont je vais parler était, voyons, j'ai dû la voir au début ou au milieu des années 1970. C'était une performance présentée au 112 Greene Street. Et cela se passait le soir. C'était à l'époque où le 112 était un lieu très à la mode, et je me souviens qu'on voyait beaucoup de peinture verte craquelée sur les murs. La performance se déroulait dans la cage d'ascenseur. L'artiste se trouvait dans la cage d'ascenseur et il allait inviter trois personnes à entrer dans l'ascenseur et à lui enfoncer des épingles dans le corps.

Je trouvais cela très bizarre, mais je pense que ce qui était étrange, c'était qu'il y avait beaucoup de monde – je ne sais pas combien, peut-être 50 ou 60 personnes. Et ce qui m'a frappé le plus, je crois, c'est la réaction de l'assistance. Parce que la cage d'ascenseur avait l'air, elle avait cette peinture verdâtre typique des vieux lofts et aussi une sorte de petite fenêtre, je me rappelle avoir vu une sorte de – je n'ai jamais vu vraiment la personne à l'intérieur. Peut-être l'ai-je vue, je pense étendue sur une table ou quelque chose du genre, portant seulement un pantalon. À travers la fenêtre. Et il y avait une sorte de gardien à la porte qui disait que nous ne pouvions pas entrer, mais que nous pouvions regarder par la fenêtre. Cela rappelait un peu une chambre d'exécution. J'ai pensé alors que j'étais en train de regarder quelque chose de très étrange.

Mais les gens semblaient plutôt d'humeur à fêter ; cela m'a fait penser à une ambiance de carnaval. Je veux dire, les gens avaient du vin et ils se tenaient là en se demandant quand la performance allait commencer et qui allait entrer dans l'ascenseur et passer à l'action, et les gens plaisantaient en disant : mais qu'est-ce qui se passe si on lui enfonce des épingles dans l'oeil ou bien dans les testicules, enfin, ils se demandaient : où vont-ils enfoncer les épingles, qui va le faire ? (rire) Et je ne me souviens plus des détails exactement, mais il me semblait que nous étions là depuis une bonne heure et que les gens devenaient vraiment impatients. Je voyais que les gens commençaient à en avoir marre de devoir rester debout à attendre. Non pas qu'ils devenaient turbulents, mais cela ressemblait un peu à un spectacle de carnaval. Moi je pensais : qu'est-ce que je fais ici ? Pourquoi j'ai besoin de regarder ça, de voir quelqu'un se faire enfoncer des épingles ?

Et puis quelqu'un a dit, ça y est, on va commencer, et tout le monde voulait absolument être choisi pour y aller et le faire. Et alors, tout d'un coup, ils ouvrent la porte et je me souviens que des gens ont dit « ses amis sont ici, ses amis sont ici ». Et là, des gens ont dit : tout est organisé à l'avance, il ne va laisser rentrer que quelques amis, comme ça ils vont lui enfoncer des épingles dans les doigts ou ailleurs, ils ne vont pas les enfoncer dans ses yeux. Je veux dire (rire), c'était vraiment une drôle de réaction, et ensuite, la porte s'est ouverte et quelqu'un est entré puis est ressorti, et puis quelqu'un d'autre est entré et l'a fait, et personne n'a jamais vu où les épingles avaient été enfoncées, ni de quelle façon. Et c'était tout! C'était très décevant, au sens où il ne s'est rien produit de dramatique. Mais j'imagine que la raison pour laquelle j'évoque cette performance, c'est que j'y ai pensé pendant longtemps en me demandant de quoi il s'agissait. Et je suppose que la vraie question était : de quoi il ne s'agissait pas. Je pense que si elle m'est restée longtemps en mémoire, c'est qu'il ne s'agissait pas d'une sorte d'esthétisation des objets, j'imagine qu'il était question de tension, de l'espace psychologique créé par les gens invités à pénétrer le corps de cette personne, le danger impliqué, le côté éphémère de la chose qui aurait pu, je crois, mal tourner. Mais tout s'est bien déroulé, je suppose.

Mais toute la chose provoque toujours un questionnement chez moi, sur ce qui pousse les gens… en tant que sculpture, cette idée de darder quelqu'un de petites épingles. Je continue de penser que c'était assez puissant. Imaginez quelqu'un faisant cela aujourd'hui – ça pourrait être fatal, on penserait au risque du SIDA, à toutes sortes de contaminations. Il est probable que le facteur de risque augmenterait considérablement.

FEMALE VOICE

It was a big deal at the time, and very scandalous, and … was sort of the … beginning of body art. And … I was very annoyed by it when I heard about it, what it was going to be. And the surprising thing about it is when I got to the gallery that it was in, which might have been the Reese Paley Gallery, I can't quite remember, or possibly Paula Cooper, I can't remember, that I just loved it. I wasn't annoyed by it. I thought it was really fun. And it was a … Since it had gotten so much … attention before it actually was installed, because it was an installation piece with a live performance, and… there were a lot of people there to see this on a Saturday, you know, the Saturday-going-around-to-look-at-art-thing. And …so it was a wooden structure that took up half the gallery that was…it started at the floor level of the gallery and then … I think it was just plain plywood that went up to, maybe, a height that, maybe, five or six feet into the corner of one of the galleries, that covered almost a good third of the gallery. And … sort of when you came in it was right in front of you. The gallery, at that point, if it was Reese Paley, I think it was just one big room with very high ceilings. And … the person was … under the plywood …. masturbating. And, you know, I thought that, I thought like I would be … that this is so … you know, sort of like male, another example of male glorification, self-glorification. But I … or that it would somehow be repulsive or something. But mainly I couldn't see the guy and there was this plywood thing that was sort of satisfying, a satisfying structure in itself. And there was sort of like a party atmosphere. So everyone was … was sort of celebratory … and …you know, as I think about it now in this moment, I guess …you know, the act itself is sort of celebratory, life-affirming. And …

That's all I really remember. I remember it was a very big up. And I was very surprised by it. And … it was somehow engaging, even though the person wasn't there, you know, for you to see. It was … it was really great. And I also like the aspect of the person, the artist … sort of putting himself out there in a very human way. This is very, all, all my reactions were very unexpected to me.

VOIX DE FEMME

Cela a créé beaucoup de remous à l'époque, tout un scandale, et ... c'était un peu le ... début du body art. *Et ... j'étais très irritée quand j'en ai entendu parler, de ce qui allait se passer. Et ce qui m'a surprise, c'est quand je suis allée à la galerie où c'était présentée, ça aurait pu être la Reese Paley Gallery, je ne me souviens pas exactement ou peut-être Paula Cooper je ne m'en souviens pas, j'ai tout simplement adoré. Ça ne m'a pas du tout énervé. J'ai trouvé que c'était vraiment amusant. Et c'était ... Comme on en avait tellement...parler avant même de la présenter, parce que c'était une installation qui impliquait une performance en direct et ... il y avait beaucoup de gens qui étaient venus la voir un samedi, enfin ... elle faisait partie de leur tournée des galeries du samedi, quoi. Et ... donc c'était une structure en bois qui occupait la moitié de la galerie qui était ... elle partait du sol et puis ... elle était en contreplaqué je pense, sa hauteur devait être d'un mètre cinquante ou un mètre quatre-vingts environ (cinq ou six pieds), dans le coin de l'une des salles, qui recouvrait presque un bon tiers de la galerie. Et ... placée de telle façon que dès qu'on entrait, on se trouvait face à elle. Quant à la galerie, si c'était Reese Paley, je crois qu'il y avait juste une grande salle avec de très hauts plafonds. Et ... la personne était ... en-dessous du contreplaqué ... occupée à se masturber. Et je pensais que, enfin je croyais que je serais ... que c'était quelque chose de ..., enfin vous savez, quelque chose de typiquement masculin, un autre exemple de glorification masculine, d'auto-glorification. Mais je ... ou que je trouverais cela dégoûtant ou quelque chose du genre. Mais surtout, je ne pouvais pas voir le gars et il y avait cet élément en contreplaqué qui avait un certain sens, qui était une structure acceptable en soi. Et il y avait un peu une ambiance de fête. Donc, tout le monde était ... était un peu en train de célébrer ... et, enfin, en y réfléchissant en ce moment précis, je pense ..., vous savez, que l'acte lui-même tient de la célébration, de l'affirmation de la vie. Et ...*

C'est tout ce dont je me rappelle vraiment. Je me souviens que cette pièce a fait beaucoup de bruit. Et que ça m'a beaucoup surprise. Et ... c'était en quelque sorte engageant, même si la personne n'était pas là, je veux dire, pas visible pour le visiteur. C'était ... c'était vraiment bien. Et j'aime aussi la démarche de la personne, de l'artiste qui ... s'exposait là de façon très humaine. C'est très ... toutes, toutes mes réactions m'ont moi-même beaucoup surprise.

Briefly describe a conceptual art work, not your own, of the period between 1965 and 1975, which you personally witnessed/experienced at the time. For the sake of this project, the definition of conceptual art should be broad enough to encompass such phenomena of that period as actions documented through drawings, photographs, film, and video; concepts executed in the form of drawings or photographs; objects where the end product is primarily a record of the precipitant concept, and performative activities which sought to question the conventions of dance and theater.

Inadequacy*

Rosalyn Deutsche

In 1989, Michael Asher participated in *L'art conceptuel: une perspective*, an exhibition that represents one of the first institutional attempts to define Conceptual Art.[1] Asher's contribution, which took the form of a proposal, was the only new work in the exhibition – all others dated from the 1960s and 1970s – and therefore the only one able to call attention to the specific circumstances of its display. Reviving the historical conceptualist practice of placing advertisements in art publications, Asher proposed that announcements of *L'art conceptuel* be taken out in various scholarly art journals, with the aim of notifying art historians "that a new historical perspective is being mapped on to conceptual practice." Asher did not oppose the historicization of Conceptual Art. On the contrary, he wrote that "historical objectification ought to be accelerated while there is still a collective experience and memory which can assist in the clarity of an analysis."[2] But, as his statement makes clear, he assumed that history bears the imprint of memory, and, what is more, he urged historians to proceed self-reflexively, "simultaneously opening up a space to ask fundamental questions regarding history making."[3] Silvia Kolbowski did not know about Asher's work, but nearly ten years later, in a project titled *an inadequate history of conceptual art* (1998–1999), she responded to its call, producing just such a meta-historical space, though one opened up in a work of art rather than an art-historical text.

Unaware of Conceptual Art during its heyday, and her student years, in the late 1960s and 1970s, Kolbowski approached it later, by way of psychoanalysis and feminism. By the early 1980s, she belonged to an interdisciplinary group of feminists who were developing a psychoanalytically informed critique of subjectivity in representation, and she was exhibiting with a group of artists who likewise turned toward the subject, challenging myths of visual purity and disinterested vision by exploring the image as a site of unconscious investments and investigating the role played by vision – looking at images – in establishing and maintaining hierarchies of sexual difference.[4] Of course, the feminist critique of vision was interwoven with conceptualist strategies, so much so that one critic, reviewing *Difference: On Sexuality and Representation*,[5] an early exhibition of art informed by psychoanalytic feminist ideas about vision and sexuality, and one in which Kolbowski took part, wrote that "there hasn't been such a purely Conceptual art exhibition in New York museums since the summer of

*Excerpts reprinted by permission of the author.

21

1970." In fact, she continued, "in feminism, Conceptualism may have found its greatest and most urgent subject."[6] Yet Kolbowski's direct encounter with historical Conceptual Art was belated: "What was decisive for me in moving away from abstract, by then monochromatic, painting around 1976 was my growing engagement with feminism," she recalls.

> This shift, together with my growing interest in psychoanalytic theory, and my engagement with some of the strategies referred to as appropriationist in the 1980s, resulted in photographic work like the *Model Pleasure* series, which I produced starting in 1982. But toward the late eighties, I began to question the way in which this work was displayed; in other words, I was not satisfied with its matter-of-fact placement on the walls of galleries and museums....So in the mid-to-late 1980s, I read whatever texts I could find on historical Conceptualism. I was interested in earlier attempts to deal with the spatial aspects of institutions, of natural and urban settings, and of display conventions.[7]

Kolbowski's path to Conceptual Art is manifest in *an inadequate history of conceptual art,* for, I want to argue, the work views Conceptual Art – or, more precisely, contemporary histories of Conceptual Art – within the perspective of subsequent artistic developments and, in particular, through a feminist lens. Not just because it includes female voices; not just because it defines Conceptual Art in terms intended, as Kolbowski puts it, "to allow for an inscription of women artists" into the movement's history;[8] but also, and most significantly, because, in keeping with the wish of a certain kind of feminism, it pleads for what Jacqueline Rose calls an "ethics of failure"– a wish announced by the word "inadequate" in the work's title.[9] "Inadequate" does not function here as a derogatory adjective, one that indicates the presence of deficiencies that can and must be corrected if Kolbowski's account of the artistic past is going to measure up to an ideal of complete, which is to say, adequate historical knowledge. Rather, inadequate describes the condition of all cultural histories, since history is a representation of – a narrative about – the past and therefore unequal to reality. It does not correspond to things as they were. And narrativity is inadequate for another reason: it arises from desire, a desire, as Hayden White says, introducing the problem of subjectivity into the writing of history, "to have real events display the coherence, integrity, fullness, and closure of an image of life that is and can only be imaginary."[10]

"Inadequate" functions interrogatively as well as descriptively in Kolbowski's title, questioning from a feminist standpoint not only the possibility but the very ideal of historical adequacy or completeness. For if, as Joan Wallach Scott wrote in the 1980s, women's history has offered "a critique of history that characterized it not simply as an incomplete record of the past but as a participant in the production of knowledge that legitimized the exclusion or subordination of women,"[11] feminists have since argued that historical knowledge performs this legitimizing role most effectively precisely when it claims completeness, when, that is, it disavows failure. In the absence of an a priori, unifying ground of history, one deriving from a source outside the social world, completeness can only be achieved through a gesture of exclusion, an elimination of otherness that affirms and at the same time prevents history's cohesiveness. When, however, historians refer to a substantive foundation that totalizes history and generates the limits of their narratives, they justify and conceal their exclusions, rendering them invisible and withdrawing them from the terrain of contestation. Kolbowski's history, by contrast, insists on its own inadequacy and, in doing so, stresses the importance of acknowledging rather than overcoming the failure of representational adequacy, insofar as history fails when, opening itself to the voices of others, it questions the rhetorical certainties of its reception of the past. Hence, inadequacy's ethico-political dimension.

Kolbowski made *an inadequate history* as a contribution to, and commentary on, a rediscovery of Conceptual Art that began more than a decade ago. An early sign of the rediscovery was the appearance of the term "neo-conceptualism," which has since settled into the vocabulary of art discourse, where it is used loosely to categorize diverse, even ideologically opposing, art practices – those of Kolbowski included – that mobilize the movement's principal signifiers – amateur photographs, texts, diagrams, appropriation, pastiche – and thus have a conceptualist look. In addition, major exhibitions of Conceptual Art, accompanied by scholarly catalogues, spanned the 1990s, inaugurated in Paris by *L'art conceptuel, une perspective,* whose purpose was to build "something like a history of Conceptual Art."[12] In 1996, the Los Angeles Museum of Contemporary Art mounted *Reconsidering the Object of Art: 1965–1975,* which was followed in 1999 by *Global Conceptualism: Points of Origin, 1950s–1980s* at the Queens Museum in New York.[13] Anthologies, monographs, and collections of documents appeared.[14] Lucy Lippard's classic record of the movement, first published in 1973, was reprinted.[15] And art historians undertook the task of historicizing Conceptual Art. Two of the most important histories are Benjamin Buchloh's highly influential "Conceptual Art 1962–1969: From the Aesthetic of Administration to the Critique of Institutions," written for the Paris exhibition catalogue, and Alexander Alberro's *Conceptual Art and the Politics of Publicity,* which, published in 2003, postdates *an inadequate history* and thus demonstrates the ongoing relevance of Kolbowski's work.[16]

The return to Conceptual Art contains diverse tendencies. One, exemplified by the term "neo-conceptualism," treats the movement largely in terms of style and therefore detaches it from its radical history. "It seemed like this return was just too smooth and fast,"[17] says Kolbowski, who, against the superficiality of this aspect of the return, emphasizes the historicity of Conceptual Art while still remaining open to the possibility of its contemporary relevance as an aesthetically and politically radical practice. She hopes, as Simon Leung does, that Conceptual Art might be "returned to criticality, and continued beyond a reproduction of spectacles and effects."[18]

The return to Conceptual Art has, of course, produced less superficial histories, among which at least two orientations can be distinguished.[19] *Global Conceptualism*, for one, exemplified the tendency to expand the movement to embrace broad chronological periods – the 1950s–1980s – as well as a wide range of international artists working in a conceptualist manner. It produced a cultural history that, while significant for its openness to non-canonical artists and otherwise marginalized groups, offers illusions of plenitude and thus runs the risk of fostering a type of pluralism that neutralizes differences, in the sense of antagonisms, within the field of Conceptual Art, thereby doing away with the dimension of the political. A second approach is taken in recent accounts of Conceptual Art written by art historians whose desire to historicize Conceptual practices goes hand in hand with the mobilization of historical-materialist modes of cultural analysis that use the discourse of political economy to draw the line between the political and non-political. Like Kolbowski, these writers stress Conceptual Art's historical and political character but, unlike Kolbowski, they drastically restrict the movement's scope, tightening its temporal and geographical borders in what can seem like an attempt to assuage any uncertainty of definition. One might say that they go too far in the opposite direction from global conceptualism, for some of the most theoretically rigorous materialist histories, while extremely valuable in their complexity and difference from neutralizing accounts, prompt serious reservations, since they are uncompromisingly androcentric, building canons of Conceptual Art that eliminate women. Of equal, if not greater concern is the fact that they ignore contemporary feminist challenges to totalizing visions of art, politics, and history and, against these challenges, eliminate otherness from all three, pushing sexuality to the back of the aesthetic, political, and historical mind. To be sure, art historians sometimes acknowledge the absence of women and, more rarely, of feminism from their histories. In fact, such caveats have become quite common in introductions to books about contemporary art in general, where they tend to minimize, even while admitting to omissions, which, since the absence of a topic can be the first clue to its presence, actually structure these art histories....

. . . . . .

...*An inadequate history* responds to current accounts of Conceptual Art by introducing memory – and with it, the unconscious mind – into the writing of history.

In 1998, adopting a conceptualist practice, Kolbowski asked sixty artists to follow a set of directions:

> Briefly describe a conceptual art work, not your own, of the period between 1965 and 1975, which you personally witnessed/experienced at the time. For the sake of this project, the definition of conceptual art should be broad enough to encompass such phenomena of that period as actions documented through drawings, photographs, film, and video; concepts executed in the form of drawings or photographs; objects where the end product is primarily a record of the precipitant concept, and performative activities which sought to question the conventions of dance and theater.

She requested that they speak solely from memory, conduct no research, and reveal neither their own identities nor those of the artists and works they recalled. Forty artists agreed to produce such inadequate accounts, and in the end Kolbowski tape-recorded twenty-two stories. As the artists spoke, she also videotaped their hands, focusing attention on the very element of art-making that Conceptual Art wanted to do away with: the hand of the artist.

The result, a record of the artist's own precipitant concept, was a kind of performance first staged by Kolbowski in 1999 at American Fine Arts Co., a New York gallery with two adjacent exhibition spaces. On a wall in the gallery's front room, Kolbowski projected a nine-by-twelve-foot silent video loop showing enlarged close-ups of the artists' moving, gesturing hands. On the same wall in the back room, she played the acoustic loop of the artists' stories, which she had arranged chronologically according to the dates of the conceptual artworks that the artists described, or, rather, the dates as the artists remembered them, which in some cases are wrong, as a printed sheet distributed in the gallery informed viewers. The handout also listed the participants, but individual voices and hands remained anonymous. The two components of the installation – sound and image – were de-synchronized so that any individual artist's voice was heard in conjunction with an image of the hands of a different artist. Because of this disjunction and because, for technical reasons, Kolbowski used only half of the video footage, thereby making the audiotape twice as long as the video, hands frequently changed in the middle of a spoken testimony; or vice-versa: a new testimony began but hands remained the same. Coupled with the physical division of the gallery, the inability to connect sound and image, to locate them in a single person, placed the viewer in an ungrounded space, depriving her of the centered, distanced position of full knowledge from which to receive the work, the artists' "testimonies," or, for that matter, the past, which was never available as a totality.

The acoustic recording unfolded on a sleek Bang & Olufsen Beosound 9000 CD player, whose advertising slogan, Kolbowski later revealed, asserts that the player is "Created. Not made,"[20] a claim echoing what may be the most common description of Conceptual Art: An art of ideas. Not handmade objects. However, the CD player did not stand for Conceptual Art itself but for the superficial, mechanical aspect of its current rediscovery. For, as Alberro astutely observes, the "slickly designed, state-of-the-art Bang & Olufsen" actually differs from Conceptual Art, contrasting sharply with an "artmaking practice that dreamed of democratizing the realm of the aesthetic by employing low-tech materials." And this difference corresponds to another: that between historical Conceptual Art and its current rediscovery, between, that is, "a previously iconoclastic artistic movement and its return in a new historical context," where it has become "a catchall that has little to do with the rigorous definitions of the original movement."[21]

The soundtrack of *an inadequate history*, on which the artists tell their stories about Conceptual Art, highlights the difficulties that beset memory: falsifications, gaps, repressions, displacements, and denials. What is remembered has also fallen into oblivion. Mnemonic uncertainties surface on the level of thematic content as speakers acknowledge the inadequacies of their accounts. Almost no one claims accuracy. One speaker inquires into the motivations of memory and forgetting, wondering why a *particular* work has stuck in her mind. Another is simply "stuck," bereft of anything more to say. Several voices equivocate about what they saw or where they were when they saw it. Exact dates or locations cannot be recalled or are misremembered. One speaker brings to the fore the question of memory by recalling a work *about* memory, while another alludes to an accidental head injury that occurred just before she viewed the work, making her memory "*still* a little peculiar," a statement that casts doubt on the ordinariness of any memory. A few stories seem rehearsed – maybe as a protest against what is perceived as the control of the questioner or as a defense against material that might unwittingly erupt in memory. One artist, describing a work by Michael Asher, doubts whether it took place. "I heard about this piece," she says, "but you know, it maybe even wasn't done." Perhaps disingenuous, her professed uncertainty nonetheless illuminates memory's tricks.

Uncertainty is not confined to content, however. Slips of the tongue, laughter, stuttering, stumbling repetitions, and throat-clearing and other afflictions of the voice also disrupt the coherence of the artist's stories, functioning like metonyms of *an inadequate history*'s broader attempt to disrupt or, as Kolbowski puts it, "slow down" the historicization of Conceptualism. Various kinds of otherness eliminated from dominant histories reappear – multiplicity, voices of women, the voice of feminism, and the unconscious or otherness within.

Originally published in *Silvia Kolbowski: inadequate...
Like...Power* (Vienna: Secession and Cologne: Verlag
der Buchhandlung Walther König, 2004).

ROSALYN DEUTSCHE is an art historian and critic who teaches
at Barnard College in New York City. She is the author of
Evictions: Art and Spatial Politics, MIT Press, 1996.

Notes

1   *L'art conceptuel, une perspective* (Paris: Musée d'Art Moderne de la Ville de Paris, 1999).

2   The full text of Asher's proposal is: "*L'art conceptuel, une perspective* is as much a view of Conceptual Art as it is a perspective of the institutions used for the maintenance and historical production of that practice. What are the forces and conditions driving the historical analysis which are beyond conceptual art practices own definition of its historical context and production procedures? Historical objectification ought to be accelerated while there is still a collective experience and memory which can assist in the clarity of an analysis, simultaneously opening up a space to ask fundamental questions regarding history making. To look at this question further, I propose as my contribution to *L'art conceptuel, une perspective* that separate groups of historians be notified by an announcement of this exhibition in the below journals that a new historical perspective is being mapped on to conceptual art practice. *M.A. Apollo, Art History, Daidalos, The Journal of Aesthetic and Art Criticism, La Revue du Louvre et des musées de France, Romagna Arte e Storia*, and *Simiolus*."

3   *Ibid.*

4   The artists included Victor Burgin, Sarah Charlesworth, Mary Kelly, Sherrie Levine, Cindy Sherman, Gretchen Bender, Louise Lawler, and Laurie Simmons, among others. In mounting a feminist critique of vision, these artists also questioned theories of postmodernism, which at that point remained indifferent to sexuality and gender. On this blindness, see Jane Weinstock, "A Laugh, A Lass and a Lad," *Art in America*, 71:6 (Summer 1983), 8; and Craig Owens, "The Discourse of Others: Feminists and

Postmodernism," in Hal Foster, ed., *The Anti-Aesthetic: Essays on Postmodern Culture* (Port Townsend, Washington: Bay Press, 1983), 57–82.

5   "Difference: On Representation and Sexuality," organized by Kate Linker and Jane Weinstock (New York: New Museum of Contemporary Art, 1985).

6   Roberta Smith, "Beyond Gender," *The Village Voice*, January 22, 1985, 103.

7   Simon Leung, "Contemporary Returns to Conceptual Art: Renée Green, Silvia Kolbowski, and Stephen Prina, *Art Journal* (Summer 2001), 57–58.

8   Quoted in Mignon Nixon, "*She-Fox*: Transference and the 'Woman Artist,' " in *Women Artists at the Millennium*, Carol Armstrong and Catherine de Zegher, eds. (Cambridge: MIT Press/October Books, 2006).

9   Jacqueline Rose, *Why War?–Psychoanalysis, Politics, and the Return to Melanie Klein* (Oxford, UK and Cambridge, MA: Blackwell, 1993), 36.

10   Hayden White, "The Value of Narrativity in the Representation of Reality," *Critical Inquiry* 7:1 (Fall 1980).

11   Joan Wallach Scott, *Gender and the Politics of History* (New York: Columbia University Press, 1988) 26.

12   Claude Gintz, " '*L'art conceptuel, une perspective*': Notes on an Exhibition Project," in *L'art conceptuel, une perspective, op.cit.*, 19.

13   *Global Conceptualism: Points of Origin, 1950s–1980s* (Queens: The Queens Museum of Art, 1999); *Reconsidering the Object of Art: 1965–1975* (Los Angeles: The Museum of Contemporary Art, 1996).

14   See, for example, Alexander Alberro and Blake Stimson, eds., *Conceptual Art: A Critical Anthology* (Cambridge, MA: MIT Press, 1999; Peter Osborne, *Conceptual Art* (London: Phaidon Press, 2002); and *Michael* Corris, ed., *Conceptual Art: Theory, Myth, and Practice* (Cambridge: Cambridge University Press, 2004).

15   Lucy Lippard, *Six Years: The Dematerialization of the Art Object from 1966 to 1972* (Berkeley: University of California Press, 1997).

16   Alexander Alberro, *Conceptual Art and the Politics of Publicity* (Cambridge, MA: MIT Press, 2003); "Conceptual Art 1962–1969: From the Aesthetic of Administration to the Critique of Institutions," *October* 55 (Winter 1990).

17   Leung, *op.cit.*, 66, and in conversation with the author, November 12, 2003.

18   Leung, *op.cit.,* 54.

19   For another description of these two tendencies, see Paul Wood's discussion of the term "conceptualism" in his *Conceptual Art* (New York: Delano Greenridge Editions, 2002), 8–9.

20   Quoted in Kolbowski, "an inadequate history of conceptual art," *October* 92 (Spring 2000), 53.

21   Alexander Alberro, "Silvia Kolbowski," Artforum 38:4 (December 1999), 148–149.

Inadéquation*

Rosalyn Deutsche

En 1989, Michael Asher participait à l'exposition *L'art conceptuel : une perspective* qui représente l'une des premières tentatives officielles de définir l'art conceptuel[1]. Sous forme d'une proposition, la contribution de Asher était l'unique œuvre nouvellement créée – toutes les autres œuvres datant des années 1960 et 1970 – et, dès lors, la seule vraiment susceptible d'attirer l'attention sur les circonstances spécifiques de sa présentation. Ravivant la coutume de l'art conceptuel consistant à placer des annonces publicitaires dans des publications sur l'art, Asher proposait d'insérer dans plusieurs revues d'art spécialisées des annonces sur *L'art conceptuel* dans le but de signifier aux historiens de l'art qu'«une nouvelle perspective historique se dessinait pour la pratique conceptuelle». Asher ne s'opposait pas à l'historicisation de l'art conceptuel allant, au contraire, jusqu'à écrire «[qu'] il fallait accélérer l'objectivation historique tant que subsistaient l'expérience et la mémoire collective susceptibles de contribuer à la clarté d'une analyse[2].» Mais, comme sa déclaration le précise, il supposait que l'histoire porte la trace de la mémoire et, de surcroît, exhortait les historiens à procéder de manière autoréflexive, «en ouvrant en même temps un nouvel espace où l'on pose des questions fondamentales sur la fabrication de l'histoire[3].» Silvia Kolbowski ignorait l'existence de cette œuvre mais, une dizaine d'années plus tard, elle a répondu à l'appel d'Asher dans un projet intitulé *an inadequate history of conceptual art* (1998–1999) où elle réalisait justement un espace métahistorique de ce type, même si c'était dans une œuvre d'art plutôt que dans un texte d'histoire de l'art.

N'ayant pas connaissance de l'art conceptuel, ni au moment de son élaboration, ni pendant ses études à la fin des années 1960 et durant les années 1970, Kolbowski l'abordera plus tard, par l'entremise de la psychanalyse et du féminisme. Au début des années 1980, elle faisait partie d'un groupe interdisciplinaire de féministes qui s'attachait à développer une critique de la subjectivité dans la représentation fondée sur la psychanalyse et, en compagnie d'autres artistes intéressés par le sujet, elle présentait des œuvres qui remettaient en question les mythes de la pureté visuelle et du regard neutre en explorant l'image comme un lieu d'investissement inconscient et en examinant comment la vision – le regard sur l'image – contribue à établir et à maintenir les hiérarchies instaurées par la différence sexuelle[4]. La critique posée par les féministes sur le regard s'entrecroisait évidemment avec des stratégies conceptualistes, à tel point qu'après avoir

*Extraits reproduits avec l'aimable permission de l'auteur.

31

vu *Difference: On Sexuality and Representation*[5], l'une des premières expositions à rassembler des œuvres d'art – dont certaines de Kolbowski – abordant le thème de la vision et de la sexualité sur la base d'une vision psychanalytique féministe, une critique d'art écrivait que «les musées de New York n'avaient pas présentés une exposition d'art aussi strictement conceptuel depuis l'été 1970». C'est même «dans le féminisme, poursuivait-elle, que le conceptualisme pourrait avoir trouvé son sujet le plus important et le plus urgent[6]». Pourtant, le contact direct de Kolbowski avec l'art conceptuel historique allait se produire plus tard : «L'événement décisif qui m'a poussée à me détourner de l'art abstrait et à renoncer à peindre des monochromes tels que j'en réalisais autour de 1976 a été mon engagement croissant dans le féminisme», se souvient l'artiste :

> Ce sont cette nouvelle orientation, ainsi que mon intérêt de plus en plus marqué pour la théorie psychanalytique et ma décision d'opter pour des stratégies «appropriationnistes» dans les années 1980, qui m'ont amenée à réaliser un travail photographique donnant lieu, entre autres, à la série *Model Pleasure*, débutée en 1982. Mais, vers la fin des années 1980, j'ai commencé à m'interroger sur la façon dont ce travail était présenté ; en d'autres termes, son accrochage tel quel sur les murs des galeries et des musées ne me satisfaisait pas […]. Vers le début, le milieu et la fin des années 1980, j'ai donc entrepris de lire tout ce que je pouvais trouver sur le conceptualisme historique, en m'intéressant aux premières tentatives de traiter les questions d'espace relatives aux institutions, aux environnements naturels et urbains et aux modes établis de présentation[7].

an inadequate history of conceptual art nous renseigne très clairement sur la voie qui a mené Kolbowski à l'art conceptuel : selon moi, il est indéniable que cette œuvre examine l'art conceptuel – ou plus précisément les histoires contemporaines de l'art conceptuel – dans la perspective des développements artistiques ultérieurs et, plus spécifiquement, à travers le prisme du féminisme. Pas seulement parce qu'elle inclut des voix de femmes ; pas seulement parce qu'elle définit l'art conceptuel en termes destinés à, comme l'explique Kolbowski, «permettre aux femmes artistes de s'inscrire» dans l'histoire du mouvement[8] ; mais aussi et avant tout parce qu'en restant en phase avec le désir exprimé par un certain type de féminisme, l'œuvre plaide pour ce que Jacqueline Rose nomme une «éthique de l'échec» – un désir signifié par l'emploi du mot «*inadequate*» dans le titre de l'œuvre[9]. «*Inadequate*» n'est pas utilisé ici comme un qualificatif péjoratif destiné à attirer l'attention sur la présence de déficiences qui peuvent et doivent se corriger au cas où l'on confronte le rapport de Kolbowski sur le passé de l'art à un idéal de connaissance historique intégrale, c'est-à-dire adéquate. Le mot indique plutôt la condition propre à toutes les histoires culturelles, puisque l'histoire est une représentation – ou une narration – du passé forcément inégale à la réalité. Elle ne correspond pas aux choses telles qu'elles étaient. Mais il y a une autre raison à l'inadéquation de la narrativité : celle-ci provient du désir, comme le dit Hayden White en posant le problème de la subjectivité dans l'écriture de l'histoire, de « voir les événements réels présenter la cohérence, l'intégrité, la plénitude et l'aboutissement d'une image de la vie qui n'est et ne peut être qu'imaginaire[10]. »

Kolbowski se sert du mot « inadéquat » aussi bien de manière interrogative que descriptive, en questionnant d'un point de vue féministe non seulement la possibilité de l'adéquation ou de l'aboutissement historique, mais l'idéal même que cela représente. Car, si l'histoire des femmes, comme le notait Joan Wallach dans les années 1980, a proposé « une critique de l'histoire montrant que non seulement celle-ci était un récit incomplet du passé, mais qu'elle contribuait aussi à produire un savoir qui légitimait l'exclusion ou la subordination des femmes »[11], des féministes ont depuis lors affirmé que c'est précisément quand ce savoir prétend à la totalité, c'est-à-dire quand il récuse l'échec, qu'il joue ce rôle de légitimation historique avec le plus d'efficacité. En l'absence d'un fondement a priori capable d'harmoniser l'histoire et venu d'une source extérieure au monde social, la totalité ne peut s'obtenir qu'au prix d'un geste d'exclusion, d'une élimination de l'altérité qui affirme et empêche en même temps la cohérence de l'histoire. Mais lorsque les historiens font référence à un fondement essentiel qui englobe l'histoire et génère les limites de leurs récits, ils justifient et dissimulent leurs exclusions, en les rendant invisibles et en les soustrayant de la zone de contradiction. L'histoire de Kolbowski insiste au contraire sur sa propre inadéquation et, du coup, sur l'importance de reconnaître plutôt que de maîtriser l'échec de la représentation adéquate, pour autant que l'histoire échoue lorsque, s'ouvrant aux voix des autres, elle questionne les certitudes rhétoriques de sa réception du passé. D'où la dimension éthique et politique de l'inadéquation.

Kolbowksi a réalisé *an inadequate history*, en l'envisageant comme une contribution à et un commentaire sur la redécouverte de l'art conceptuel qui s'était amorcée il y a plus de dix ans. Un des premiers signes de cette redécouverte a été l'apparition du terme « néoconceptualisme » désormais implanté dans le vocabulaire du discours sur l'art où il sert de manière assez libre à désigner des pratiques artistiques diverses, voire idéologiquement opposées – y compris celle de Kolbowski – qui font appel aux signifiants principaux du mouvement – photographies amateurs, textes, diagrammes, appropriation, pastiche – et revêtent du coup une allure conceptualiste. Il faut y ajouter l'éclosion d'expositions majeures sur l'art conceptuel qui a marqué les années 1990 et donné lieu à la publication de catalogues érudits ; la première du genre, intitulée *L'art conceptuel, une perspective* et présentée à Paris, visait à «construire quelque chose comme une histoire de l'art conceptuel[12].» En 1996, le Los Angeles Museum of Contemporary Art organisait l'exposition *Reconsidering the Object of Art: 1965–1975* suivie de l'exposition *Global Conceptualism: Points of Origin, 1950s–1980s*, présentée au Queens Museum de New York[13]. Plusieurs anthologies, monographies et recueils de documents voyaient le jour[14]. Paru une première fois en 1973, l'essai désormais classique que Lucy Lippard consacrait au mouvement a été réédité[15]. Par ailleurs, les historiens de l'art s'attaquèrent à l'«historicisation» de l'art conceptuel. Les deux réalisations les plus importantes allant dans ce sens sont «De l'esthétique d'administration à la critique institutionnelle (aspects de l'Art conceptuel, 1962–1969)», l'influent essai de Benjamin Buchloh pour le catalogue de l'exposition parisienne, et *Conceptual Art and the Politics of Publicity*, l'ouvrage d'Alexander Alberro qui, paru en 2003, suit de quelques années *an inadequate history* et démontre la pertinence soutenue de l'œuvre de Kolbowski[16].

Le retour à l'art conceptuel traduit la présence de plusieurs tendances. Celle qu'illustre le terme «néoconceptualisme» aborde surtout le mouvement en termes de style, le détachant par là de son histoire radicale. «Ce retour me semblait juste trop simple et trop rapide», explique Kolbowski[17] qui, à rebours du caractère superficiel de ce retour, souligne l'historicité de l'art conceptuel, sans pour autant exclure la possibilité qu'il conserve sa pertinence actuelle comme pratique esthétiquement et politiquement radicale. À l'instar de Simon Leung, elle espère que l'art conceptuel puisse «retrouvé sa dimension critique et se poursuivre au-delà d'une reproduction de spectacles et d'effets[18].»

Le retour à l'art conceptuel a évidemment inspiré des approches moins superficielles, parmi lesquelles deux orientations au moins se distinguent[19]. La première, le conceptualisme global, illustre la tendance à élargir le mouvement de manière à y englober des séquences chronologiques de longues durée – les années 1950 à 1980 – en même temps qu'un éventail important d'artistes internationaux œuvrant dans un esprit conceptualiste. Il en est résulté une histoire culturelle dont l'attention portée à des artistes moins connus et à des groupes par ailleurs marginalisés est remarquable certes, mais n'offre que l'illusion de la totalité, courant ainsi le risque de promouvoir un genre de pluralisme qui neutralise les différences – prises au sens d'antagonismes – dans le champ même de l'art conceptuel, gommant ainsi la dimension politique. Dans la seconde approche, qui caractérise plusieurs essais en histoire de l'art récemment consacrés à l'art conceptuel, les auteurs abordent l'histoire de ce mouvement avec la volonté d'historiciser les pratiques conceptuelles à partir d'une analyse culturelle fondée sur le matérialisme historique qui recourt au discours de l'économie politique pour établir la distinction entre le politique et le non politique. Comme Kolbowski, ces auteurs soulignent le caractère historique et politique de l'art conceptuel, mais contrairement à elle, ils en réduisent drastiquement la portée et en rétrécissent les limites temporelles et géographiques, suivant un mouvement qui ressemble à une tentative d'évacuer toute incertitude quant à une définition. On pourrait dire qu'ils vont trop à rebours du conceptualisme global : en effet, certaines des analyses historiques matérialistes théoriquement les plus rigoureuses, tout en se révélant d'une complexité très intéressante et loin de l'essai réducteur, suscitent de sérieuses réserves du fait qu'elles sont radicalement androcentriques et établissent des canons d'art conceptuel qui excluent les femmes. Plus préoccupante, plus inquiétante même, est leur tendance à ignorer les tentatives féministes contemporaines de questionner les visions globalisantes de l'art, de la politique et de l'histoire et à procéder à l'encontre de ces remises en question en évacuant de ces trois champs toute altérité et en refoulant la sexualité à l'arrière-plan de la réflexion esthétique, politique et historique. Il y a bien sûr certains historiens de l'art qui admettent que les femmes et, plus rarement, le féminisme sont absentes de leurs analyses. De plus en plus fréquent dans les introductions aux ouvrages sur l'art contemporain en général, ce type de mise en garde tend en fait à minimiser les omissions tout en les reconnaissant, suivant une tendance qui structure en réalité ces histoires de l'art, puisque l'absence d'un sujet peut être la première indication de sa présence. […]

. . . . . .

[…] An *inadequate history* constitue une réponse aux récits qui circulent aujourd'hui sur l'art conceptuel en introduisant la mémoire – et par là, l'inconscient – dans l'écriture de l'histoire.

En 1998, empruntant une approche conceptualiste, Kolbowski demandait à soixante artistes de suivre les directives suivantes :

Décrivez brièvement une œuvre d'art conceptuel, créée par une autre personne que vous au cours de la période allant de 1965 à 1975, dont vous avez personnellement fait l'expérience ou avez été témoin à l'époque. Aux fins de ce projet, la définition d'art conceptuel doit être suffisamment large pour inclure des phénomènes de cette époque, tels que des actions documentées par des dessins, des photographies, des films et des vidéos ; des concepts matérialisés sous forme de dessins ou de photographies ; des objets où le produit est avant tout la retombée documentaire d'un concept afférent, ainsi que des activités de performance qui visaient à remettre en question les formes établies de la danse et du théâtre.

Elle leur a demandé de s'exprimer de mémoire, de ne faire aucune recherche et de ne révéler ni leur identité ni celle des artistes et des œuvres dont ils se souvenaient. Quarante artistes ayant accepté de livrer ces comptes rendus inadéquats, Kolbowski a finalement enregistré vingt-deux récits. Pendant que les artistes parlaient, elle filmait aussi leurs mains, attirant l'attention sur cette composante du « faire » que l'art conceptuel souhaitait justement évacuer: la main de l'artiste.

Le résultat, la retombée documentaire du concept afférent, pris la forme d'une espèce de performance présentée par Kolbowski une première fois en 1999 à la galerie American Fine Arts Co. à New York, dans deux espaces d'exposition contigus. Sur l'un des murs de la salle située à l'avant, Kolbowski projetait une vidéo en boucle de grand format (274 x 365 cm) qui montrait en plan rapproché les mains des artistes relatant leur expérience. Sur le mur, dans l'autre salle située à l'arrière, était reproduite en boucle la bande-son des histoires racontées par les artistes, organisées de manière chronologique suivant les dates des œuvres conceptuelles qu'ils décrivaient ou, plus exactement, suivant les dates telles qu'ils les avaient gardées en mémoire, celles-ci étant incorrectes dans certains cas, comme le précisait une feuille imprimée distribuée aux visiteurs de la galerie. Ce document donnait aussi la liste des artistes participants au projet, mais les voix et les mains de chaque personne restaient anonymes. Les deux composantes de l'installation – le son et l'image – étaient désynchronisées de façon à faire coïncider le son de la voix de chaque artiste avec l'image des mains d'un autre artiste. À cause de cette dissociation et du fait que, pour diverses raisons techniques, Kolbowski n'avait utilisé que la moitié des séquences enregistrées – ce qui rendait la bande-son deux fois plus longue que la vidéo –, les mains changeaient souvent en plein milieu du récit ou, à l'inverse, un nouveau témoignage s'amorçait alors que les mains restaient en place. Confrontés simultanément à la division de la galerie en deux espaces, à l'incapacité de relier le son à l'image, de les faire coïncider en une seule personne, le visiteur se retrouvait dans un espace déstabilisé. Il ou elle se retrouvait incapable d'assumer la position centrée et distancée lui permettant de saisir pleinement l'œuvre, les « témoignages » des artistes ou, en l'occurence, le passé qui n'a jamais pu s'appréhender comme une totalité.

L'enregistrement sonore était diffusé sur un élégant lecteur audio Bang & Olufsen Beosound 9000 CD dont l'annonce publicitaire affirmait, comme Kolbowski le précisera plus tard[20], que ce lecteur est « Créé. Non fabriqué », une affirmation faisant écho à ce qui est sans doute la description la plus courante de l'art conceptuel : un art des idées. Et non d'objets faits à la main. Cependant, le lecteur CD ne représentait pas l'art conceptuel lui-même, mais l'aspect mécanique superficiel de la redécouverte actuelle du mouvement.

En effet, comme le remarque finement Alberro, «le design ultramoderne et à la fine pointe de la technologie du lecteur Bang & Olufsen» est très éloigné de l'art conceptuel et contraste fortement avec une «pratique artistique qui rêvait de démocratiser le champ de l'esthétique en utilisant des matériaux rudimentaires». Et cette différence renvoie à une autre, celle qui existe entre l'art conceptuel historique et sa version actuelle redécouverte, c'est-à-dire entre «un mouvement artistique d'abord iconoclaste et son retour dans un nouveau contexte historique», où il est devenu «un fourre-tout qui n'a plus grand-chose à voir avec les définitions rigoureuses du mouvement original[21].»

La bande sonore de *an inadequate history*, sur laquelle les artistes racontent leurs histoires sur l'art conceptuel, met en évidence toutes les difficultés que renferment la mémoire, à savoir les falsifications, les trous, les refoulements, les déplacements et les dénis. Ce qui est remémoré est également tombé dans l'oubli. Des incertitudes mnémoniques remontent à la surface du contenu thématique alors que les locuteurs reconnaissent l'inexactitude de leurs récits. Presque aucun d'entre eux ne revendique l'exactitude. Une participante s'interroge sur les motivations de la mémoire et de l'oubli, se demandant pourquoi elle a gardé le souvenir d'une œuvre en particulier. Une autre est tout simplement «bloquée», incapable de continuer son récit. Plusieurs «voix» émettent des doutes sur la nature de ce qu'elles ont vu ou sur l'endroit exact où elles se trouvaient lorsqu'elles l'ont vu. Certains n'arrivent pas à se souvenir exactement de la date ou de l'endroit ou bien s'en souviennent incorrectement. Une personne attire l'attention sur la question de la mémoire en se remémorant une œuvre qui avait la mémoire pour thème; une autre artiste explique qu'une blessure à la tête encourue accidentellement juste avant de voir l'œuvre rend le souvenir qu'elle en garde «toujours un peu étrange», semant par là le doute sur la dimension ordinaire de tout souvenir quel qu'il soit. Quelques histoires donnent l'impression d'avoir été répétées, en réaction peut-être au contrôle exercé par Kolbowski que certains ont perçu ou pour se protéger de souvenirs qui pourraient remonter à la surface involontairement. Alors qu'elle décrit une œuvre de Michael Asher, une artiste doute même que la performance ait réellement eu lieu. «J'ai entendu parler de cette œuvre», dit-elle, «mais vous savez, elle n'a peut-être jamais été réalisée». Sincère ou non, son incertitude avouée n'en éclaire pas moins les tours que nous joue notre mémoire.

Mais l'incertitude ne se limite pas au contenu : lapsus, rires, balbutiements, hésitations, râclements de gorge et autres affectations de la voix entravent eux aussi la cohérence des récits et renvoient par métonymie à l'objectif plus large visé par *an inadequate history*, à savoir perturber ou, pour reprendre les termes de Kolbowski, «ralentir» l'historicisation du conceptualisme.

Toutes sortes d'altérité éliminées des histoires dominantes font leur réapparition – la multiplicité, les voix des femmes, la voix du féminisme avec la part d'inconscient ou d'altérité qui s'y loge.

Traduit de l'anglais par Marine Van Hoof.
Paru dans *Silvia Kolbowski: inadequate... Like... Power*, Vienne, Secession et Cologne, Verlag der Buchhandlung Walther König, 2004.

ROSALYN DEUTSCHE est historienne de l'art et enseigne au Barnard College, New York. Elle est l'auteure de *Eviction: Art and Spatial Politics*, MIT Press, 1996.

Notes

1   *L'art conceptuel, une perspective*, Paris, Musée d'Art Moderne de la Ville de Paris, 1989.

2   Le texte intégral de la proposition de Asher se lit comme suit : « L'art conceptuel, une perspective est aussi bien une vision de l'art conceptuel qu'une mise en perspective des institutions utilisées pour le maintien et la production historique de cette pratique. Quelles sont les forces et les conditions guidant l'analyse historique qui existent au-delà de la définition du contexte historique et des processus de production que donnent les pratiques artistiques conceptuelles ? Il faudrait accélérer l'objectivation historique tant qu'il subsiste encore une expérience et une mémoire collectives qui peuvent contribuer à une analyse claire tout en ouvrant un espace où l'on pose les questions fondamentales sur la production de l'histoire. Pour étudier ce problème plus à fond, je suggère comme contribution à *L'art conceptuel, une perspective* d'informer des groupes indépendants d'historiens par le biais d'une annonce sur cette exposition publiée dans les journaux ci-dessous que la pratique de l'art conceptuel fait l'objet d'une nouvelle mise en perspective historique. *M.A. Apollo, Art History, Daidalos, The Journal of Aesthetic and Art Criticism, La Revue du Louvre et des musées de France, Romagna Arte e Storia* et *Simiolus*. »

3   *Ibid.*

4   La liste de artistes invités incluait entre autres Victor Burgin, Sarah Charlesworth, Mary Kelly, Sherrie Levine, Cindy Sherman, Gretchen Bender, Louise Lawler et Laurie Simmons. En développant une critique féministe de la vision, ces artistes remettaient aussi en question les théories postmodernistes restées jusque là indifférentes à la sexualité et au genre. Au sujet de cette cécité, voir Jane Weinstock, « A Laugh, A Lass and a Lad », *Art in America*, vol. 71, nº 6 (été 1983), p.8 et Craig Owens, « The Discourse of Others: Feminists and Postmodernism », dans Hal Foster (sous la dir. de), *The Anti-Aesthetic: Essays on Postmodern Culture*, Port Townsend, Washington, Bay Press, 1983, p. 57–82.

5   *Difference: On Representation and Sexuality*, commissaires : Kate Linker et Jane Weinstock, New York, New Museum of Contemporary Art, 1985.

6   Roberta Smith, « Beyond Gender », *The Village Voice*, 22 janvier 1985, p. 103.

7   Simon Leung, « Contemporary Returns to Conceptual Art: Renée Green, Silvia Kolbowski, and Stephen Prina », *Art Journal* (été 2001), p. 57–58.

8   Cité dans Mignon Nixon, « She-Fox: Transference and the 'Woman Artist' » dans *Women Artists at the Millenium*, Carol Armstrong et Catherine de Zegher (sous la dir. de), Cambridge, MIT Press/October Books, 2006.

9   Jacqueline Rose, *Why War? – Psychoanalysis, Politics, and the Return to Melanie Klein*, Oxford, R.-U., et Cambridge, MA, Blackwell, p. 36.

10 Hayden White, « The Value of Narrativity in the Representation of Reality », *Critical Inquiry,* vol 7, n° 1 (automne 1980).

11 Joan Wallach Scott, *Gender and the Politics of History*, New York, Columbia University Press, 1988, p. 26.

12 Claude Gintz, « "L'art conceptuel, une perspective" : Notes sur un projet d'exposition » dans *L'art conceptuel, une perspective, op.cit.*, p.19.

13 *Global Conceptualism: Points of Origin, 1950s–1980s*, Queens, The Queens Museum of Art, 1999 ; *Reconsidering the Object of Art: 1965–1975*, Los Angeles, The Museum of Contemporary Art, 1996.

14 Voir entre autres Alexander Alberro et Blake Stimson (sous la dir. de), *Conceptual Art: A Critical Anthology*, Cambridge, MA, MIT Press, 1999; Peter Osborne, *Conceptual Art*, Londres, Phaidon Press, 2002 et Michael Corris (sous la dir. de), *Conceptual Art: Theory, Myth, and Practice*, Cambridge, R.-U., Cambridge University Press, 2004.

15 Lucy Lippard (sous la dir. de), *Six Years: The Dematerialization of the Art Object from 1966 to 1972*, Berkeley, University of California Press, 1997.

16 Alexander Alberro, *Conceptual Art and the Politics of Publicity*, Cambridge, MA, MIT Press, 2003 ; « Conceptual Art 1962–1969: From the Aesthetic of Administration to the Critique of Institutions », *October* 55 (hiver 1990).

17 Leung, *op.cit.*, p. 66, et dans une conversation avec l'auteure, le 12 novembre 2003.

18 Leung, *op.cit.*, p. 54.

19 Pour une autre description de ces deux tendances, voir la manière dont Paul Wood conçoit le terme « conceptualisme » dans son ouvrage *Conceptual Art*, New York, Delano Greenridge Editions, 2002, p.8–9.

20 Cité par Kolbowski dans « an inadequate history of conceptual art », *October* 92 (printemps 2000), p.53.

21 Alexander Alberro, « Silvia Kolbowski », *Artforum,* vol. 38 n° 4 (décembre, 1999), p. 148–149.

Models of Intervention:
A Discussion between
Michèle Thériault and
Silvia Kolbowski

MICHÈLE THÉRIAULT: Both *an inadequate history of conceptual art* (*aihca*) and *After Hiroshima Mon Amour* (*AHMA*) take historical moments, entities, events – a period in art and an approach to art making called conceptual art and a film that reflects on the cataclysm that was Hiroshima, namely Alain Resnais's *Hiroshima mon amour* (1959) – and recasts them into the "here and now." Both projects do this in such ways as to makes us reconsider the "then and there" and how it extends, transforms, and is transformed by, the present. There is a continuous mise-en-abyme in both works, because they continuously weave in and out of the past and the present, concerned as they are with the myriad ways that the past meets the present and vice versa. However different these two works are, they form a reflection on history and historicization that is founded on disjunction. Disjunction – and the multiple points of views that arise from it – seems crucial to how history intersects with contemporary life for you and in your desire to address history in these works.

SILVIA KOLBOWSKI: "How the past meets the present and vice versa" are of great importance to me. The reciprocity that you point out is all-important, because of the fluidity with which the psyche forms an understanding of the world we inhabit. In other words, the past is filtered through the present, and the present is filtered through the past, which involves psychical processes such as identification, projection, and displacement. There has been a tendency, at least in the U.S., to separate out "history" and the political present from such psychical processes. I think this is a big mistake on the part of academics, not to mention journalists, pundits, and politicians. For example, how governments solicit compliance with regard to policies that are so clearly detrimental to society is not something that can be understood without understanding these processes.

So in this way I guess one could say that *aihca* is a "case history" that takes into account both how we historicize a particular moment of aesthetic production, as well as how we historicize the past in general.

With regard to *AHMA*, Resnais himself was at pains to point out that what people referred to as cinematic and narrative "flashbacks" in *Hiroshima mon amour* were not actually flashbacks, because he considered them to be memories experienced *in the present* by the characters. That was a very provocative comment for him to make, because it is a point of view that insists on the mutability of the past. That is, all histories are mediated through the present, or one could say that they move backward and forward through time, and are not affixed rigidly to a time-line. This view does not, in my opinion, undermine the necessity to understand historical facts and events as connected to a particular moment as well. Historicity matters, but it is more complex than just finalizing data on a timeline.

As for disjunction, coming of age as an artist in the 1980s I absorbed the legacies of early 19th century Modernism as well as the tenets of cultural post-modernism in the U.S. And in both instances, disjunction played a methodological part. For me, disjunction is important in various ways. I suppose I do still believe, although it may not be a popular view at a moment when linear narrative is privileged, in the modernist notion that disjunction creates a more engaged spectator. But it has other subtle effects as well. Recently I screened *AHMA* in Poland, and the art historian Agata Jakubowska pointed out something very interesting to me. She said that when she read a particular title in the video – "This could only happen in one city. Hiroshima." – and the image that was lined up with the title clearly showed a street in Iraq (or somewhere in an militarily-occupied middle eastern country), rather than Hiroshima, the misalignment of words and image created a space for her to project another – a Polish – city, or cities, into the space created by the disjunction. She noted that in general the disjunctions between titles and images in the video allowed for trans-geographic and trans-historical entry (projection, identification?). To me, this was a very important comment, given how reluctant Poland has been to look at its own history as aggressor, passive bystander, and victim.

MT: It is striking to me how much both works are paradoxically constructed around a visual absence, and that lack is an important part of the visitor's experience when encountering these works. For instance in *aihca* one never "sees" the conceptual artwork described by each person based on what they remember. In *AHMA*, as war and love are juxtaposed, direct aggression, a nuclear explosion, and the act of lovemaking are never seen. Is their absence replaced by their presence as inscriptions in history? Is seeing/sight in this process wholly inadequate? How do you see its status in the context of remembrance and trauma?

SK: On the one hand, the absence is a methodological strategy. The omission of the referent allows the spectator some space for projection and reflection that is at least partially anchored by the spoken and written language that I include (so that meaning is open, but not completely open-ended). The speakers in *aihca* are referring to specific artworks, but due to my request that they not refresh their memories, the speaker does not occupy a position of certainty, and in turn the spectator of the project occupies a position that is in a way parallel to that of the speaker. The spectator hears the speaker trying to recall an experience of an artwork from memory, and can try to formulate an image or experience of the work in their minds. In this sense, the perception of time, and what time does to memory and knowledge, becomes part of the spectator's experience. I hope there is always a sensation of doubt with regard to that process, so that many things can be placed in doubt – including the unilateral assumptions of much historicization.

In *AHMA*, I am paralleling the strategies of Resnais and Duras in *Hiroshima mon amour* in their incorporation of several potent omissions. You could say that *Hiroshima mon amour* deals with the ethics of representation through omission, by blocking ready cinematic identification in scenes involving only limbs of naked bodies, as well as scenes where there are no reverse shots, a strategy which creates a complex form of identification for the spectator. Resnais and Duras create a spectator who has to come to terms with various moral dilemmas that the film represents – i.e. what role does the psyche play in recasting the past? In what ways can such cataclysmic suffering *and, importantly, its aftermath,* be represented? How can one gain knowledge of an event that was meant to obliterate life? And where does one position oneself, as a spectator, in terms of national and cultural legacies and present ethical transgressions?

In basing my work on theirs, I wanted to raise questions for the contemporary spectator that resonate with these earlier questions. Resnais and Duras took on the challenge of excavating the aftermath of a morally unjustifiable attack that caused death and suffering to hundreds of thousands of people. The dropping of the two nuclear bombs on Japan were carried out in full knowledge – at least by the U.S. government – that the Japanese were willing to surrender, and did, in fact, eventually surrender on the same terms that were offered before the bombs were dropped. The spectators of my video are witness to – in the media and as citizens – unjustified incursions into places like Iraq and Afghanistan, and witness to the passive violence to which New Orleans and its impoverished inhabitants have been subjected.

But interestingly, in light of your question, I think that there is also a kind of surplus, an excess, of the visual in *AHMA*. This excess takes the form of not only the unnaturalistic colors in some scenes, but also takes the form of using 10 actors to play the two actors of *Hiroshima mon amour,* and casting actors who are of various ethnicities and racialities. So the spectator has to deal with a visual excess that may result in a questioning of cultural assumptions based on visuality. In a way, in *AHMA*, there is too much to see.

On a personal note, I have a different kind of connection to the absence of the visual. Having been taken out of my country of birth at the age of 6, and having returned there only four times in the subsequent 48 years, I've lived with mostly mental images of formative childhood experiences of places and people. Being wrested from that culture was most definitely a traumatic experience, so one could say that the obsession with the absence of the visual has both historical and personal meanings for me.

MT: To follow through on the subject of visual excess and omission, I can think of another paradoxical manifestation of it. It is in the use of the projected video image on a large scale. A large-scale video image is always already an apparatus of visual excess to which the viewer and the artist can be easily subsumed. It is increasingly difficult to work *with* video, as opposed to video *working* you, the artist. In the light of the importance in these two works of what escapes the visual, cannot be captured by it, and your continuous investigation of a realm that lies outside of it, how do you negotiate "working with video"?

SK: In my first two projects that incorporated video, in 1996 and 1997, I worked with small monitors because I couldn't rationalize presenting the video on a bigger scale, other than to compete with large-scale painting, or cinematic impact. I was determined, in each instance, to use a scale of projection/presentation that was appropriate to the work, rather than increasing the scale to that of the museum or gallery room, which was quite prevalent then. I ended up with the sense that the small scale I used did not satisfy the contemporaneous spectatorial and curatorial appetite for large-scale projections.

But in historical terms I still could not rationalize moving to a bigger scale just to make the work appealing. With *aihca*, in the late '90s I moved to larger scale projection because I did not want the hands in the work to be presented in a scale that was naturalistic. And I wanted the scale of the projected hands to contrast with the small but concentrated materiality of the Bang & Olufsen CD player in the adjoining room. So I blew the hands up to a monumental scale, which also magnifies the expressive aspects of the hands – the signs of aging that situate the speakers historically, the hypnotic gestural movements. And it exaggerates a visual pun, where the hands stand in for the missing artists, and for the missing visual information on the artworks.

With *AHMA* my reasons for projecting the work at a large scale are two-fold. The large scale allows the spectator to feel drawn into the narrative of the video, to become implicated in an almost bodily sense by it. Painting the walls of the projection space in a color that is found in the video (as I did at LA><ART in Los Angeles, and as is the case at the Ellen Gallery) extends the space of the video and envelopes the spectator within the "image," so to speak.

The large scale of the *AHMA* projection (although at about 11 feet across, it is fairly modest by contemporary standards) allows for a perceptual advantage that I only noticed when I first viewed the video at a scale larger than the monitor scale at which it was edited and reviewed during post-production. At monitor-scale, my sense is that the spectator struggles somewhat to take in the titles – which are almost constant – simultaneous with the moving imagery. At a large scale, the spectator can comprehend the meaning of the titles while absorbing the signification of the moving imagery in an almost atmospheric manner. I'm sure it has something to do with the ways in which the brain takes in visual and textual cues and meaning at the same time, and I was somewhat surprised to see that the spectator's capacity for absorbing the quasi-narrative was so much improved through a large-scale projection.

That said, although I do consider the scale of projection carefully in my work, there exists a kind of unspoken pressure to produce installations at a visually impactful scale, and ideally with a captivating twist in the projection format. I think this exists for several reasons. On the one hand, artists have been competing with Hollywood's amazing computerized special effects since at least the '80s, and also with the popular appeal of large-scale painting, sculpture, and photography as they appear in increasingly large-scale museums, at least in an American culture where bigger is seen as better. It will be interesting to see the impact on time-based art of the proliferation of tiny-screen mass distribution (i.e. downloadable movies and TV shows), because there's a generation that seems to not distinguish too much between the scales of projection, while privileging narrative content.

MT: Both *aihca* and *AHMA* point to important shifts in art making, filmmaking and writing that occurred in the 20th century. In *aihca,* the redefinition of the terms of art making represented by Conceptual art is the underlying substance around which the work evolves. In *AHMA*, your focus in working off Resnais's film is not to reassess the new forms of visual and textual narrative that it introduced and came to so beautifully exemplify. However, you nevertheless make full use of the flashbacks that slice through the film, joining past and present, and of the disembodied and fragmented narrative of the screenplay and dialogues that draws together as it separates, to enable in your video the coexistence of multiples points of views and of the public and private realms. Just as these two installations shift between the past and the present, how do you, today (in the current art world), position yourself in relation to these radical attempts to rethink the conventions of art making, filmmaking and textual narrative?

SK: For me, methodology and subject matter are inextricably bound together. The politics of representation are as important as the representation of politics. This is why I find both Conceptualism and the Resnais/Duras film to be so interesting. In historical Conceptual work of the '60s and '70s there is an attention to the ways in which meaning is produced – whether through art's association with institutional contexts and mediums (museums, galleries, magazines, discursive commentary, the paratextual, etc.) or through a kind of deconstruction of sites of enunciation (for example, through the displacement from conventional mediums to performative ones, where the body takes the place of the art object).

I was, and continue to be, fascinated by the ways in which the past is interwoven with the present in *Hiroshima mon amour*. Resnais utilized specifically filmic strategies and vocabularies that are very interesting to me – the ways in which the camera positions the spectator, the particular uses of montage to blur the boundaries between time frames, the use of music as both a voice and a way of "coloring" the imagery, the alternation of newsreel footage and narrative footage, the disconnection of voice from image through framing, so that in the early section you're not sure whether the bodies framed by the camera are connected to the voices heard simultaneously on the soundtrack. And these approaches are representational strategies that can't be disconnected from the script. Duras's script itself formulates a way of working with language, time, memory, trauma, and questions of ethical responsibility that Resnais then visualizes, and *augments*, through filmic strategies. It's not a flawless film, in that Resnais and Duras had their historical blind spots, but I find it fascinating how in this instance it was not a case of a filmmaker instrumentalizing a script produced a priori by a writer, but a very enmeshed collaboration. Form and narrative – it's hard to tell where one ends and the other begins in terms of the way meaning is created in *Hiroshima mon amour*.

As for how I position myself in relation to these earlier strategies, I would say that I'm not iconoclastic in my approach, meaning that I gladly welcome whatever legacies are still relevant for the present moment. My focus is on what might be meaningful to contribute to a dense world of images and sounds. I have never really understood the need on the part of some artists to "kill the father," so to speak. Or the mother, for that matter. That goal seems impoverishing to me, unless such a paradigm shift would be capable of allowing us to consider differently the social conventions that we take for granted.

MT: I am interested in the reach of your comment "… what might be meaningful to contribute to a dense world of images and sounds." When we met in New York, you said to me at one point that you had more than once considered stopping making art. I was impressed by your candor and actually felt for some time after the weight of your comment's implications, the seriousness of it. And that for me is tied to the nature of your work. Every single work you have realized has been carefully researched, and seems to come to be after what appears at times a long process of honing, of subtle adjustments to get it right as if this subtraction or that addition will determine that "meaningfulness". It appears to be a difficult and meticulous process that signals to me a kind of *prise de position*. I would like to link this to a concern with ethics that marks your practice. You spoke of an ethics of representation earlier in relation to what Resnais omits visually from *Hiroshima mon amour*. Rosalyn Deutsche, in her essay "Inadequacy,"[1] refers to Jacqueline Rose's "ethics of failure" as a productive frame for the "inadequacy" in your project on Conceptual art. And you state in a short text reproduced in this volume that *AHMA* offers to the spectator "the possibility of ethical inquiry".

SK: I think that my response to the way in which the art field and the art market "blew up" in the late '80s was to reduce my output, rather than increase it. Given my age, I caught the tail end of an art scene in New York that was dramatically smaller than it is now. That scale created a sense of meaningful exchange – between artists, between artists and critics, and between artists and audiences. And I was also fortunate enough to come of age in the early '80s when appropriationist art had permeated an extended network of academic and social discourses and publications. So I experienced a more intimate scene in which one could mount an exhibition and actually feel like it was making a contribution to critical exchanges and discourses.

That experience dropped away in the late '80s due to a focus on the market and object making. And because of the market growth and the media attention this created, graduate degree programs in fine arts proliferated, as well as a kind of gold-rush attitude on the part of young students/artists (and sometimes their tuition-paying or rent-subsidizing parents) who saw it as a field that might be financially viable rather than marginal. It started to be thought of as a calculated economic risk. Frankly, I knew then and I know now that dizzying financial rewards in the art field are few and far between. But that fantasy dies hard. In any case, that shift had a destabilizing effect on me. It became impossible to feel like one's contributions to the field and to audiences had much meaning, or to work at an individual pace that wasn't geared to the market and its networks – fairs, galleries, etc. I wasn't calculating about producing less, but it just felt better to exhibit work less frequently than to get caught up in a whirlwind of endless group exhibitions and a myriad of gallery shows. Later I ran across a comment that Duchamp made toward the end of his life when he was asked how he felt about Warhol's work. He said that he found the work interesting, but that the main difference between he and Warhol was that Warhol always tried to make as much work as possible, while he tried to make as little as possible. Two models!

I think a second profoundly destabilizing moment occurred for me around 2004, when it was intensely apparent that the havoc that the Bush administration was wreaking was pervasive on a global scale, and resistance was difficult.

In both instances, the question raised for me was how an artist could possibly intervene in the face of the instrumentalization and degradation of so many lives. I think that the honing process you refer to is the attempt to craft a publicly meaningful response to this kind of overwhelming power. There is no surety in the process, which involves trying to understand what sort of audience the work creates. For me, the taking of a position as an artist has to involve visual, aural, and written languages that are not common to other disciplines. Otherwise, why not just move into those disciplines? There should be something we can glean from art that is different than what we can glean from all other fields. And recently I have been wondering whether electoral politics haven't become quite useless in precipitating needed change, therefore making cultural contributions more important. It might seem odd that I'm saying this as Obama is about to be inaugurated as President, but given most of the appointments he's made to his cabinet, it's hard to feel hopeful about electoral politics providing something other than a site of discourse. That's certainly not nothing, but it is confusing given that the rhetoric around this presidency-elect concerns pragmatic action above all in the face of the mess that the Bush administration has left behind.

What I mean by an ethics of absence in *Hiroshima mon amour* has to do with the ethics of the camera to a large extent – what Resnais chooses to show or not show of the suffering of others and of the ways in which cultures record such suffering. He is also precise about where the visual point of view is at a given moment in the film. That is an ethical decision, because a visual point of view so often makes the spectator feel the certainty of commanding an image. But those choices are also inextricably bound to absences in the script. What the characters don't say is as important as what they do say, and what their *affect* conveys without speaking. And language is also important for a film that had to deal with the difficulty of connecting two cultures with different experiences of a traumatic and evitable event, the dropping of the atomic bomb on Japan.

In *AHMA* I initially used a French language voiceover for the whole video (with English titles). But I was never comfortable with that voiceover, and after months of editing I realized that the video was lacking silence. That's why it now has English titles and only one short scene with a French voiceover. Of course, while silence and absence can sometimes be used in an ethical manner, lack of action is can also be very aggressive, as in the case of New Orleans, or in protecting residents of Iraq.

MT: Do you think *aihca* provides a form of ethical inquiry about the intermittent manifestations of conceptual art during the past half-century, as manifested in the ways this art is remembered?

SK: I began the *aihca* project in order to try to slow down a process of historicization that was proving to be quite fast and narrow. It's not to say that a methodology that slows down historicization is always an ethical one, but in this instance I think that the inclusion of certain practices that had been overlooked is valuable. Why leave out performative and filmic/video work, as some historians and curators had done? In doing so, most of the women artists who worked at that time were left out. Was there an anxiety about having the performative, the body, "feminize" the history of conceptual art? But the project was also an attempt to slow down the process enough to question the mechanisms by which histories come to be validated. The process inscribed a questioning of authority in the authoring of historicization. This is emphasized through the anonymity of the speakers in the project – who were artists, not professional critics – as well as the inclusion of faulty memories, and my literal silence in the work. This is what Deutsche and Mignon Nixon[2] took up in their analyses of the project, in part through Rose's concept of the "ethics of failure," and in part through psychoanalytic concepts. A historicization of events and movements that does not take into account displacements, projections, screen memories, etc., seems to me to be problematic, if an ethical approach can be considered, at least in part, to involve an understanding of how "otherness" is created…

MT: You commented in an interview with Hal Foster on spectatorial passivity and on ways to counter that. And you stated your dislike of bringing story and body together, finding manipulative an overemphasis on personal experience in art and media.[3] I think you want an "active" spectator/exhibition visitor who not only physically moves between here and there (the audio and the images of the hands being situated in different rooms in *aihca*), but whose senses are also brought forcefully into play in the experience of the work (for example, in *AHMA*, the richly saturated colors of the military action sequences interspersed with the shimmering, luminescent intertwined bodies of *she* and *he*; the silence followed by the hard and invasive sounds of the military actions; or the disembodied ring of each speaker's voice in *aihac* in relation to our *embodied* listening of it; the insistent presence of touch in both). And a spectator whose cultural assumptions are tested (the various actors and actresses of indeterminate race and ethnicity who play the couple in *AHMA*). I could go on, there are so many permutations of this fracturing that creates, as you say earlier in this interview, "a more engaged spectator", a more critical one.

I find it fascinating how the body and the "story" are in a sense irrevocably and inextricably linked, but at the same time are kept apart in these two installations. The coming together of the two are kept in check as they permeate the space of the exhibition and our experience of the two works.

SK: That's a very interesting parallel that you draw. I had not been consciously aware of the fracturing qualities in *AHMA* as produced by the contrasts of silence and sound, and saturated color and non-color, etc. While I had intended the disjunctions between the Duras synopsis/dialogue and Resnais' montage in relation to the contemporary imagery I culled, I hadn't thought about it as paralleling the fracturing in *aihca*. I would have to agree that it's fascinating how the coming together of body and the story are kept in check. Now, if I only had a little more control over such thinking as I was making the work…!

MT: I'd like to end this discussion on a question about exhibition contexts. The critical nature of your practice has always reflected simultaneously upon the apparatus of presentation and representation of the society of which you're a part, and the apparatus of your work – your art making –

in that society. That includes, of course, the apparatus of the art world). Many of your projects have directly questioned the status, function, or site of exhibition (*Enlarged from the catalogue: the United States of America,* 1988; *An example of recent work ...* 1990; *Enlarged from the catalogue: Michael Asher ...*, 1990; *Once more with feeling,* 1992; *These goods are available at* _____, 1995; *Like the difference between ...*, 1995). Clearly, the exhibition site, space and context shaped the specificity of the work. In the interview with Foster you state that some of those projects could not be done today; they would be unreadable because the changing aesthetics of display styles and marketing techniques have blurred the boundaries between the culture of consumption and of art. And the legibility that you desire for your work required you to rethink your strategies and techniques as they intersected with the public realm, resulting in your readjusting your work process. You describe developing a "more detached work process that could make [you] less subject to endless cultural permutations, while still letting [you] remain alert to cultural and political events." *aihca* and *AHMA* are projects in which, as you say: "the exhibition site became virtually unimportant, and in some ways the institution did too, except with regard to history (for *aihca*)."[4] That is quite a statement and a shift. Does that mean that a critique of the space and institution of exhibition is no longer possible, or that it has been superseded by a more pressing critique? Or has the nature (the rich transhistorical content and visual and aural means of presentation) and imperatives of these two installations shifted to another site or transformed your relationship with the spectator and the institutional space?

SK: There is a primary importance for me, as an artist, in being able to make an environment for myself in which I can actually be creative and produce work. A painter may focus on the physical space of the studio and its light, but for a post-studio artist the "studio" is the world, to some extent. And the world is harder to regulate than the studio! With "An example of recent work may be seen in the windows of Harry Winston, Inc…" I was able to start a series of inexpensive projects situated in various cities, without getting the approval of city governments and officials (which had frustrated me in the late 1980s). I did this by using the paratextual elements of exhibitions to direct spectators to sites, and sometimes around cities. So I by-passed the censorship normally imposed by nervous officials; often artists engage in self-censorship even before a project gets to the approval process. I also devised a class that I taught for many years, in which art and architecture students were required to develop budget-less projects that addressed and were situated in various sites in the cities in which I taught.

The "workaround" projects of this period helped me to create a form of exhibition space that was specific, unregulated, and uncommissioned. But the rituals of perception in cities started to change dramatically in the 1990s. The melding of design, display, art, advertising, and technology grew to be overwhelming. So I moved on to more internally reflective works that made their own environments, so to speak. It was a way of moving back to the gallery or museum without having to wait for commissions, without dealing with "white cube" issues. Because, after all, how many times can you foreground the "white cube" for spectators? The critical elements did get more internalized in the work. Using time-based work allowed me to do this more easily. I'm still sensitive to issues of installation and the situatedness of the embodied spectator. But I focus less on the mechanics of institutional signification because I noticed in the early part of this decade that the strategies of revelation and exposure at play in a lot of "institutional critique" were not making anyone uncomfortable. Like the blasé public attitudes of this decade toward certain practices – torture, rendition, illegal invasion, the transgression of constitutional rights, and government corruption – the exposure of complicities in relation to art institutions was not rattling anyone. So while I value enormously the legacies of institutional critique, it seemed a good time to move on to different approaches. The world is an intensely complex place today – the wielding of power is both more brutal and more subtle than it's ever been. And understanding our imbrication in this spectrum is quite a challenge. I feel fortunate to have a métier through which to comment, as well as feel my way through.

Notes

1   Rosalyn Deutsche, "Inadequacy," *Silvia Kolbowski: inadequate...Like...Power*
     (Vienna: Secession and Cologne: Verlag der Buchhandlung Walther König, 2004).

2   Mignon Nixon, "On the Couch," *October* 113 (Summer), 2005.

3   "Hal Foster Interviews Silvia Kolbowski," *Silvia Kolbowski: inadequate...Like...Power*
     (Vienna: Secession and Cologne: Verlag der Buchhandlung Walther König, 2004).

4   "Hal Foster Interviews Silvia Kolbowski," *ibid.,* p. 163–165.

P. 53–68: *After Hiroshima Mon Amour* (2008).

REALISATION

DIRECTED BY
SILVIA KOLBOWSKI
ALAIN RESNAIS

Impossible to talk

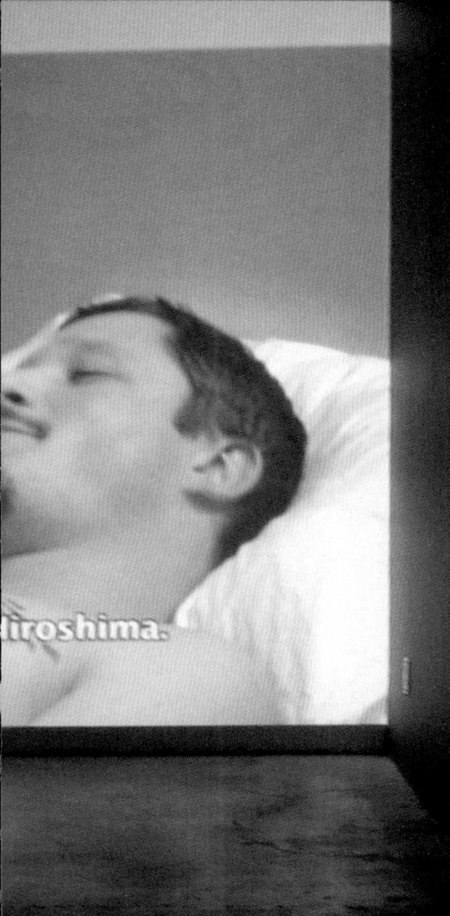
iroshima.

I saw everything. Everything.

And suddenly she appears completely dressed,
as a Red Cross nurse.

An entire city rises up in anger.

After Hiroshima Mon Amour (2008)

Silvia Kolbowski

Developed over a three-year period (2005–2008), *After Hiroshima Mon Amour* was begun with the intention to look at sites of American military incursion and governmental neglect through the lens of the celebrated 1959 film *Hiroshima mon amour*, directed by Alain Resnais and written by Marguerite Duras. *After Hiroshima Mon Amour* uses various visual and aural strategies to layer and analyze instances of violence and trauma. Titles, silence, brief sync sound, and music are used to create a new story out of an old one. The allegorical couple of the 1959 film is played by ten interconnecting actors who blur distinctions of ethnicity, race, and gender, undermining the categories that are often used to rationalize violence. And as in the Resnais/Duras film, eroticism and violence are interwoven. Various scenes in black and white are faithfully recreated from *Hiroshima mon amour*, contemporary material downloaded from the Internet is included, a remix of the score and sound design of the original becomes a "character" in the video, and color appears at inappropriate moments.

By using an earlier film as a palimpsest onto which layers are added, the contemporary focus on Iraq and New Orleans, post-Hurricane Katrina, rests on an earlier traumatic incursion and site of criminal neglect.

After Hiroshima Mon Amour (2008)

Silvia Kolbowski

Conçu entre 2005 et 2008, *After Hiroshima Mon Amour* est né d'une volonté d'examiner les enjeux des incursions militaires américaines et de la négligence gouvernementale qui en a découlé par le truchement d'une relecture du film *Hiroshima mon amour* (1959) d'Alain Resnais, d'après un scénario de Marguerite Duras. *After Hiroshima Mon Amour* a recours à diverses stratégies visuelles et orales pour décomposer et analyser des occurrences de violence et de traumatismes. Titres, silence, sons synchrones brefs et musique sont utilisés pour créer un nouveau récit à partir d'un ancien. Les rôles du couple allégorique du film de 1959 sont joués par dix acteurs liés les uns aux autres, qui brouillent les définitions d'ethnicité, de race et de genre sapant les catégories qui servent souvent à rationaliser la violence. Tout comme dans le film de Resnais et Duras, érotisme et violence sont entremêlés. Certaines scènes en noir et blanc sont fidèlement recréées à partir d'*Hiroshima mon amour*, des éléments contemporains téléchargés à partir d'Internet sont ajoutés, un remix de la musique du film et de la conception sonore de l'original devient un «personnage» dans la vidéo et la couleur apparaît à des moments inopportuns.

En utilisant un film ancien comme un palimpseste auquel des couches de signification sont ajoutées, l'accent contemporain mis sur l'Irak et la Nouvelle-Orléans, après l'ouragan Katrina, repose sur une incursion traumatique antérieure et sur les lieux d'une négligence criminelle.

After and Before

Christopher Bedford

Eroticism is assenting to life even in death.
— Georges Bataille, 1957[1]

With a mounting sense of exigency as the elections draw near, critics writing
for American art journals and magazines have begun to analyze and codify
the extent of political engagement evident in contemporary art practice
today. One of the more explicit and persuasive of these engagements was an
extended review written by Hal Foster for *Artforum* of an exhibition called
"Forms of Resistance: Artists and the Desire for Social Change from 1871 to
the Present" at the Van Abbemuseum in the Netherlands. Foster begins with
the unqualified claim that one is unlikely to see an exhibition such as this at
a major museum in the United States due to the "politically restrained and
financially driven" character of these institutions.[2] The same could be said of
the fiscally-driven gallery circuit, so it should come as no surprise that
uncompromising, politically oppositional art practices with no discernable
stake, interest, or place in the commercial circus, rarely command prime real
estate in commercial publications. In this discouraging context, Silvia
Kolbowski's ambitious video and 16mm production, *After Hiroshima Mon
Amour* (2008), developed over the course of three years, represents a
welcome deviation from the norm, not least because it merits coverage in
these pages, despite existing in a realm parallel to the art market.

   The video opens with a series of violently choreographed sequences that
refuse simple analysis. Following the production credits, we are shown a
landscape of twitching, interpenetrating limbs, covered in what looks like
glittering ash, vibrating erratically and colliding in dead, uninterrupted
silence. It could be a frenzied erotic encounter, or the uncontrolled spasms
of a body – or bodies – in the grip of death; but the action is close-up,
disembodied, with insufficient context. The silence is broken abruptly by a
night vision scene of American military personnel screaming unintelligibly
as they enter a private residence, wielding automatic weapons and ordering a
cowering naked man to the ground. A woman screams. A caption appears
on the screen in unremarkable white font: "I saw everything. Everything."
Though this footage was harvested from an internet site and represents an
authentic account of military action in Iraq, the erratic camera movements and
heavy pixilation align rather unnervingly with contemporary cinematographic

techniques employed by filmmakers such as Brian De Palma (*Redacted*, 2007) to achieve the look of embedded verisimilitude.

The video then cuts back and forth between details of shimmering, agitated flesh, and the repetition of the green night vision scene with the subtitle response, "You saw nothing. Nothing." before eventually shifting to Arabic news footage of a narrow street, strewn with unidentified detritus, the implication of bodily violence registered by the saturated red monochrome of the grainy imagery. Again, the passage is accompanied by a subtitle announcing the strategies of displacement and asymmetry that play throughout Kolbowski's video: "I've always wept over the fate of Hiroshima. Always." Although the shifts from one scene to the next are jarring, even brutal in this opening sequence, and the paratextual contradictions she introduces surreal, Kolbowski maintains the thematic continuity of the video through subtle use of rhyming syntax, the structure of the aforementioned caption ("I've always wept over the fate of Hiroshima. Always.") echoing that of the previous scene: "I saw everything. Everything." Inscribed in this initial, roughly five-minute passage is the primal, image-based logic that subtends Kolbowski's video from beginning to end – a visceral, almost precognitive quality that obviates the need for didactic narration. Instead she establishes relations between images, histories and subjectivities that operate on a far more basic and persuasive level.

After Hiroshima Mon Amour is a 22-minute contraction of the French director Alain Resnais' classic account of post-war Hiroshima, *Hiroshima mon amour* (1959), which tells the story of a fleeting and consuming love affair between a French woman and a Japanese man. Although faithful to its referent on the levels of mise-en-scène, acting, and dialogue, Kolbowski's video departs from Resnais' film at the level of "remake" with found footage that directly engages the aftermath of 9/11, the ideology of American militarism abroad, and governmental neglect at home.[3] Yet, like Resnais' original, Kolbowski's video is set in Japan, adding levels of narrative disjunction to this time-based montage. The video incorporates dramatic passages rendered to replicate certain sequences from Resnais' film, as well as a re-mix of the original score, text from Marguerite Duras' original screenplay and synopsis, and found footage of American military intervention in Iraq and governmental in-action in New Orleans in the aftermath of Hurricane Katrina. The consistent asymmetry of text and image, of narration and action, and of character and actor allow the viewer to inhabit a variety of subjectivities consecutively or even simultaneously.

The most obvious result of this structure is a video that feeds on its own indeterminacy to produce meaning by prompting close, thought, demanding – with each successive cut – revisions to tentative conclusions that seemed adequate for the previous scene. Within this shifting structure, the related impulses towards violence and erotic love are paired and played against each other consistently, with both urges presented as fundamental and impervious to rational analysis. Despite this theme of fundamentality, however, the video resists a purely trans-historical stance by remaining anchored in the specificity of character, time, place, and race, all of which are emphasized throughout, not buried or glossed. As the unnamed bodies quiver in unison, oblivious to all else, so the subjectivity of the soldier is concentrated into a historically specific expression of aggressive self-preservation. Feral love and violence are, therefore, proposed as unknowable equivalents.

If Kolbowski's video has a central thematic concern, it is the primitive logic that governs the interrelated fields of violence, war, prejudice, and eroticism. Literary theorist Jacqueline Rose has written about the mysterious psycho-politics of war, asserting that its persistence through time "signals the breakdown of the nineteenth-century faith in evolution, progress, and science."[4] Quoting Gertrude Stein, Rose continues, "If everything was understood, so it was then believed, 'there would be progress and if there was progress there would not be any wars, and if there were not any wars then everything could and would be understood.'"[5] Our inability to understand and prevent war is, therefore, incontrovertible evidence of our fundamental lack of self-knowledge. Kolbowski does not presume to understand the origins or persistence of war – to answer the simple but elusive question Rose poses, 'why war?' – but *After Hiroshima Mon Amour* goes beyond didactic or diagnostic strategies to give visual form to the unknowable, and in doing so draws a psychic thread through the interrelated subjects of love, violence, prejudice, war, and militarism. This thread is not easily translated into language, but it is palpable and persuasive on the less bounded level of visual argumentation.

Though her video is essentially bifocal in its attention to the aftermath of the atomic attack on Hiroshima as seen through the lens of a love affair, and to the sinister character of American domestic and foreign policies in the wake of the World Trade Center attacks, Kolbowski uses a variety of strategies to expand the field of subjectivities included in her narrative. In effect, the video addresses not two discrete wars, but also war as a cipher. The unnamed French woman in Resnais' film is introduced in Kolbowski's remake not as a European woman with light brown hair, but rather as a black woman with close-cropped hair, an Asian woman with dark hair, a Caucasian woman with dark hair, etc., and the man identified by a caption as a Japanese man who is "an engineer or an architect" is represented in Kolbowski's video by a man of indeterminate raciality with a block of text tattooed on his chest, and in another scene by a man who looks to be of middle-eastern origin. The cognitive dissonance fostered by the asymmetry of actor and character here provokes a mode of viewing wherein no subjectivity is simply "given" but must instead be understood, processed, and conceptualized by the viewer. As we watch an intimate scene unfold, and a character's lips move silently, a caption informs us that it is "impossible to talk about Hiroshima," by which we also understand that war as a concept is beyond the bounds of conventional analysis.

Such bold claims are bolstered not by systematic argumentation, but through demonstration. One particularly shocking sequence harvested from the internet is comprised of video shot from a Humvee barreling down a street in Bagdad, indiscriminately ramming civilian vehicles and forcing them off the Humvee's path. Here, as in other instances, Kolbowski uses color – in this case violet – to inflect the spectator's engagement with the action. To suggest that the scene is formally beautiful is to flirt with obscenity since the subject matter represents such an unflinching indictment of the prejudice and entitlement that so often attends the theatre of war. Yet Kolbowski permits – even encourages – that possibility within this sequence, so that when the Humvee revs it engine and bores remorselessly on as a man runs out of the way, the beauty of the scene is rendered abject and the act of looking dirty and incriminating. Color, then, becomes a character and silent narrator; a mute call to our collective conscience.

Kolbowski subjects her narration of the affair between the French nurse and Japanese man to regular shifts in scene, language and actor, and to a variety of combative, elegantly rendered contemporary interpolations, each of which uproot the ostensibly historical narrative, and force those dramatic sequences to resonate in the present. But eventually we are returned to the primordial imagery that is the video's nebulous undercurrent. This time, the twitching masses of flesh are rendered in shades of red and black, grainy and indistinct like the surface of a silkscreen print made animate. Here, these feverish movements are overlaid with captions such as "The food of an entire city is thrown away," quotes drawn from Duras' screenplay that situate the imagery in the aftermath of nuclear holocaust. As the scene evolves, passages of light, shadow, and color appear increasingly molecular in character, as if limbs have been reduced to essential structures, cells mutating, combining, dissociating and recombining into new forms. The more elemental the imagery, the more the possibility of comprehension recedes. What was either a scene of love or agony is stripped of its index and reduced to abstraction. Simultaneously, the text becomes more pointed and polemical, reversing the terms of the video's structure and suggesting that while we may be incapable of comprehending the fundamental impulse towards violence, we are, on an intellectual level, able to disavow the principles upon which it rests: "The anger of entire cities, whether they like it or not, against the inequality set forth as a principle by certain people against other people."

It is instructive in closing to return to an important concern raised by Foster in his observation that politically-directed art broadly conceived "is often either too direct or too obscure in its articulations."[6] Mindful of this dilemma, *After Hiroshima Mon Amour*, like all of Kolbowski's most successful projects, operates bilingually, speaking in urbane, nuanced language to the field of initiates, while steering a broader audience through the radical ideas that structure her work, without shading into condescension or didacticism. Given its referent, it is inevitable that *After Hiroshima Mon Amour* prompts the spectator to remember a specific moment at the end of World War II. But Kolbowski's interpolations and displacements claim this war as both a specific instance of historical aggression and as a cipher for all wars. The impulse remains consistent, she argues, but the specific articulation varies. *After Hiroshima Mon Amour*, in its splintered, multi-focal character bears down on the transgressions of the present through the mournful lens of the past with one anxious eye trained on the future.

Originally published in *Frieze 119* (November/December 2008), 180–183.

CHRISTOPHER BEDFORD is Curator of Exhibitions at the Wexner Center for the Arts, The Ohio State University.

Notes

1   Georges Bataille, *Eroticism* (New York and London: Marion Boyars, 1987), 11.

2   Hal Foster, "Forms of Resistance," *Artforum* (January 2008), 272.

3   Though it is not essential to interpret Kolbowski's video, it should be noted that the beginning of Resnais's film relies on a similar narrative structure, with passages of love making and dialogue between the Japanese man and French woman interrupted by post-nuclear footage.

4   Jacqueline Rose, *Why War? – Psychoanalysis, Politics, and the Return to Melanie Klein* (Oxford, UK and Cambridge, USA: Blackwell, 1993), 17.

5   Rose, *op.cit.*, 17.

6   Foster, *op.cit.*, 273.

Après et avant

Christopher Bedford

De l'érotisme, il est possible de dire qu'il est
l'approbation de la vie jusque dans la mort.
—Georges Bataille[1]

Animés d'un sentiment d'urgence de plus en plus marqué à l'approche des
élections, les critiques qui collaborent à des revues et à des magazines
d'art américains ont entamé une analyse et une codification de l'étendue
de l'engagement politique qu'on peut constater dans la pratique actuelle de
l'art contemporain. L'un de ces engagements les plus explicites et
convaincants a été fourni dans un long commentaire de Hal Foster, paru
dans *Artforum*, sur une exposition intitulée « Forms of Resistance: Artists
and the Desire for Social Change from 1871 to the Present », tenue au Van
Abbemuseum aux Pays-Bas. Foster commence en affirmant sans réserve
qu'il est peu probable que pareille exposition soit présentée dans un grand
musée américain en raison du caractère « politiquement réservé et
financièrement motivé » de ces institutions[2]. On pourrait dire la même
chose du réseau constitué par les galeries, elles aussi axées sur l'argent, et
il n'est donc pas étonnant que les pratiques artistiques adoptant résolument
des positions de confrontation politique et n'ayant pas d'enjeu, d'intérêt
ou de place visible dans le circuit commercial occupent rarement une
place de choix dans les publications commerciales. Dans ce contexte
décourageant, l'ambitieuse production vidéo et en 16 mm de Silvia
Kolbowski, *After Hiroshima Mon Amour* (2008), réalisée sur une période
de trois ans, constitue un écart bienvenu de la norme, notamment parce
qu'elle se mérite un commentaire dans ces pages-ci, en dépit du fait
qu'elle existe dans un monde parallèle au marché de l'art.

La vidéo commence par un montage brutal de séquences qui ne se
prête pas d'emblée à une analyse simple. Après le générique apparaît un
paysage fait de membres convulsifs, couverts d'une sorte de cendre
scintillante, qui s'interpénètrent, se meuvent irrégulièrement et se heurtent
dans un silence total et ininterrompu. Il pourrait s'agir d'une brûlante
rencontre érotique ou des spasmes incontrôlables d'un corps, ou de corps,
aux prises avec la mort ; l'action est filmée en gros plan, désincarnée,
sans contexte qui en permettrait une lecture certaine. Le silence est

brusquement rompu par une scène de nuit au cours de laquelle des militaires américains font irruption, en hurlant de manière inintelligible, dans une résidence privée, brandissant des armes automatiques et donnant des ordres à un homme nu recroquevillé au sol. Une femme crie. En caractères blancs ordinaires, une légende en anglais apparaît à l'écran : « I saw everything. Everything. » [J'ai tout vu. Tout.] Trouvée sur un site Internet, cette séquence est le compte rendu authentique d'une action militaire menée an Iraq ; toutefois, les mouvements irréguliers de la caméra et la grande pixellisation s'apparentent de manière plutôt troublante aux techniques cinématographiques contemporaines utilisées par des cinéastes comme Brian De Palma (*Redacted*, 2007) pour obtenir l'effet de ressemblance du témoin incorporé.

La vidéo effectue des va-et-vient entre ces fragments de chair luisante, agitée, et la répétition de cette scène de nuit verdâtre avec sa réponse sous-titrée – « You saw nothing. Nothing. » [Tu n'as rien vu. Rien] – avant de finalement passer à des séquences d'actualités en arabe où l'on voit une petite rue encombrée de détritus non identifiés, dans laquelle une violence corporelle est évoquée par le monochrome d'un rouge saturé des images granuleuses. À nouveau, la séquence accompagne un sous-titre annonçant les stratégies de déplacement et l'asymétrie qui animent toute la vidéo de Kolbowski : « I've always wept over the fate of Hiroshima. Always. » [J'ai toujours pleuré sur le sort de Hiroshima. Toujours.]. Bien que, dans la première séquence, les passages d'une scène à l'autre soient discordants, même brutaux, et que les contradictions paratextuelles qu'elle introduit soient surréalistes, Kolbowski maintient une continuité thématique dans sa vidéo en recourant subtilement à une syntaxe en rime, la structure de la légende susmentionnée (« I've always wept over the fate of Hiroshima. Always. ») faisant écho à la scène précédente « I saw everything. Everything. ». Inscrite dans ce passage initial d'environ cinq minutes se trouve la logique primordiale, basée sur l'image, qui sous-tend la vidéo de Kolbowski du début à la fin : une qualité viscérale, presque pré-cognitive, qui pare au besoin de narration didactique. L'artiste établit plutôt des relations entre les images, les histoires et les subjectivités qui opèrent à un plan beaucoup plus élémentaire et convaincant.

After Hiroshima Mon Amour est une contraction de vingt-deux minutes d'un classique du cinéma français, *Hiroshima mon amour* (1959) d'Alain Resnais, un compte rendu de l'après-guerre à Hiroshima qui relate une histoire d'amour tout aussi fugace que dévorante entre une Française et un Japonais. Bien que fidèle à sa référence sur le plan de la mise en scène, du jeu et du dialogue, la vidéo de Kolbowski s'écarte du film de Resnais en tant que « remake » avec ses séquences trouvées qui abordent directement les suites du 11-Septembre, l'idéologie du militarisme américain à l'étranger et les ratages du gouvernement au pays[3]. Cependant, comme l'original de Resnais, la vidéo de Kolbowski se déroule au Japon, ce qui ajoute des niveaux de disjonction narrative au montage temporel. La vidéo incorpore des passages dramatiques, rendus de manière à reproduire certaines séquences du film de Resnais, de même qu'un remix de la trame sonore originale, des extraits du scénario et du synopsis originaux de Marguerite Duras, des séquences trouvées de l'intervention militaire américaine en Iraq et de l'inaction gouvernementale à la Nouvelle-Orléans après l'ouragan Katrina. L'asymétrie consistante du texte et de l'image, de la narration et de l'action ainsi que du personnage et de l'interprète nous permet d'habiter consécutivement, voire simultanément, une variété de subjectivités.

Conséquence la plus évidente de cette structure, la vidéo de Kolbowski se nourrit de sa propre indétermination pour produire du sens en suscitant, à chacune de ses coupures successives, une révision serrée, réfléchie, exigeante de la conclusion provisoire qui semblait appropriée à la scène précédente. Dans cette structure variable, les élans vers la violence et l'érotisme sont couplés et constamment joués l'un contre l'autre, ces deux besoins présentés comme étant fondamentaux et étanches à toute analyse rationnelle. Malgré ce thème de vérité fondamentale, la vidéo résiste toutefois à une position purement trans-historique en demeurant ancrée dans une spécificité de personnage, de temps, de lieu et de race, lesquels sont soulignés de part en part et non pas tus ou dissimulés. Comme ces corps innommés qui frémissent à l'unisson, inconscients du reste, la subjectivité du soldat se trouve concentrée dans l'expression, historiquement précise, d'un instinct agressif de préservation. L'amour et la violence sauvages sont donc proposées comme équivalents inconnaissables.

S'il y a dans la vidéo de Kolbowski une préoccupation thématique centrale, c'est bien la logique primitive qui gouverne les champs reliés que sont la violence, la guerre, les préjugés et l'érotisme. La théoricienne littéraire Jacqueline Rose a écrit sur la mystérieuse psycho-politique de la guerre, affirmant que sa persistance à travers le temps « signale l'effondrement de la croyance du XIXe siècle en l'évolution, le progrès et la science[4] ». Citant Gertrude Stein, elle poursuit : « Si tout était compris – c'est ce qu'on croyait alors – "il y aurait du progrès et s'il y avait du progrès, il n'y aurait plus de guerres, et s'il n'y avait plus de guerres, et bien tout pourrait et serait compris"[5] ». Notre incapacité de comprendre et de prévenir la guerre est donc une preuve irréfutable de notre manque fondamental de connaissance de soi. Kolbowski ne prétend pas comprendre les origines de la guerre ou sa persistance – pour répondre à la question simple mais insaisissable posée par Rose, « pourquoi la guerre ? » –, mais *After Hiroshima Mon Amour* va au-delà des stratégies didactiques ou diagnostiques pour donner une forme visuelle à l'inconnaissable et, ce faisant, elle tire un fil psychique entre les sujets connexes que sont l'amour, la violence, les préjugés, la guerre et le militarisme. Ce fil ne se traduit pas facilement en mots, mais il est tangible et convaincant sur le plan moins convenu de l'argumentation visuelle.

Bien que sa vidéo soit essentiellement bifocale dans l'attention qu'elle porte, d'une part, aux conséquences de l'attaque atomique sur Hiroshima telle que vue par l'objectif d'une histoire d'amour et, d'autre part, à l'aspect sinistre des politiques américaines sur les plans domestique et étranger dans la foulée des attaques sur le World Trade Center, Kolbowski se sert de différentes stratégies pour élargir le champ des subjectivités incluses dans son récit. Dans les faits, sa vidéo parle non pas de deux guerres individuelles, mais bien de la guerre comme symbole. La Française sans nom du film de Resnais se retrouve dans le remake de Kolbowski non pas sous les traits d'une Européenne châtain clair, mais d'une Noire aux cheveux très courts, d'une Asiatique aux cheveux foncés, d'une Blanche aux cheveux foncés, etc., et l'homme identifié dans une légende comme étant un Japonais, «ingénieur ou architecte», est représenté dans la vidéo de Kolbowski par un homme de race indéterminée avec un bloc de texte tatoué sur la poitrine et, dans une autre scène, par un homme qui semble d'origine moyen-orientale. La dissonance cognitive générée par l'asymétrie entre acteur et personnage entraîne ici une façon de voir dans laquelle aucune subjectivité n'est simplement «donnée», celle-ci devant plutôt être comprise, traitée et conceptualisée par la personne qui regarde. Pendant qu'on observe le déploiement d'une scène intime et le mouvement silencieux des lèvres d'un personnage, une légende nous dit «it is impossible to talk about Hiroshima» [il est impossible de parler de Hiroshima], ce qui nous fait également comprendre que la guerre comme concept est au-delà des limites de l'analyse conventionnelle.

Ces affirmations audacieuses sont soutenues, non par une argumentation systématique, mais par la démonstration. Une scène particulièrement choquante, prise sur Internet, montre une captation vidéo où l'on voit une Humvee foncer dans une rue de Bagdad, se ruant sans distinction parmi les véhicules civils et les forçant à lui céder le passage. Ici comme dans d'autres cas, Kolbowski utilise la couleur, le violet précisément, pour infléchir notre engagement dans l'action. Suggérer que la scène est belle formellement, c'est flirter avec l'obscénité puisque le contenu représente une accusation indéfectible des préjugés et de la notion de droit qui participent souvent du théâtre de la guerre. Toutefois, Kolbowski permet, voire encourage, cette possibilité dans la séquence, de sorte que lorsque la Humvee accélère et continue impitoyablement son avancée et qu'un homme doit s'écarter en courant, la beauté de la scène est rendue abjecte et l'acte de la regarder, sale et compromettant. La couleur devient ainsi un personnage et un narrateur muet, un appel silencieux à notre conscience collective.

Kolbowski soumet régulièrement son récit de l'aventure entre cette infirmière française et ce Japonais à des glissements entre scènes, langues et interprètes, et à une variété d'incises contemporaines, des images de combat élégamment rendues, dont chacune déracine le récit soi-disant historique et force ces séquences dramatiques à résonner dans le présent. Toutefois, nous devons finalement retourner à l'imagerie primordiale qui constitue le nébuleux courant sous-jacent de la vidéo. Cette fois-ci, les masses de chair convulsive apparaissent dans des teintes de rouge et de noir, aussi granuleuses et indistinctes que la surface d'une gravure qui s'animerait. Ici, sur ces mouvements fébriles déroulent des légendes comme « The food of an entire city is thrown away. » [La nourriture d'une ville entière est jetée.], des citations tirées du scénario de Duras qui situent les images dans la suite de l'holocauste nucléaire. Au fur et à mesure que progresse la séquence, les passages de lumière, d'ombre et de couleur semblent de plus en plus de nature moléculaire, comme si les membres avaient été réduits à des structures essentielles, à des cellules en mutation qui se combinent, se dissocient et se recombinent en de nouvelles formes. Plus les images sont élémentaires, plus elles deviennent difficiles à comprendre. Une scène d'amour ou d'agonie se voit dépouillée de son indice et réduite à l'abstraction. En même temps, le texte devient plus lourd de sous-entendus et polémique, renversant les conditions structurelles de la vidéo et suggérant que, bien que nous soyons incapables de saisir l'impulsion fondamentale qui pousse à la violence, nous sommes intellectuellement capables de désavouer les principes sur lesquels elle se fonde : « The anger of entire cities, whether they like it or not, against the inequality set forth as a principle by certain people against other people. » [La colère de villes entières, ne leur en déplaise, contre l'inégalité mis de l'avant comme principe par certaines personnes contre d'autre personnes.]

En terminant, il est instructif de revenir à un aspect important soulevé par Foster dans son observation, à savoir que, généralement, l'art à orientation politique « est souvent trop direct ou trop obscur dans ses articulations[6] ». Sensible à ce dilemme, *After Hiroshima Mon Amour*, comme tous les projets les plus réussis de Kolbowski, opère de manière bilingue, s'adressant aux initiés dans une langue urbaine et nuancée, tout en guidant un auditoire plus vaste sur le chemin des idées radicales qui structurent son œuvre, sans tomber dans la condescendance et le didactisme. Étant donné son référent, il est inévitable qu'*After Hiroshima Mon Amour* nous incite à nous rappeler un moment précis à la fin de la Seconde Guerre mondiale. Les incises et les déplacements effectués par Kolbowski revendiquent toutefois cette guerre comme étant à la fois un exemple précis d'agression historique et un symbole de toutes les guerres. L'élan est constant, avance-t-elle, mais chaque articulation précise varie. *After Hiroshima Mon Amour*, dans son aspect éclaté, à multiples points focaux, insiste sur les transgressions du présent en passant par le regard lugubre du passé et en braquant un œil inquiet sur l'avenir.

Traduit de l'anglais par Colette Tougas.
Cet article est paru dans *Frieze 119*
(novembre/décembre 2008), p. 180–183.

CHRISTOPHER BEDFORD est conservateur des expositions au Wexner Center for the Arts, Ohio State University.

Notes

1   Georges Bataille, *L'Érotisme*, Paris, Éditions de Minuit, 1957, 2004, p. 17.

2   Hal Foster, « Forms of Resistance », *Artforum* (janvier 2008), p. 272. [Notre traduction.]

3   Bien que ce ne soit pas essentiel à l'interprétation de la vidéo de Kolbowski, il faut noter que le début du film de Resnais s'appuie sur une structure narrative semblable dans laquelle les scènes érotiques et les dialogues entre le Japonais et la Française sont interrompus par des séquences post-nucléaires.

4   Jacqueline Rose, *Why War? – Psychoanalysis, Politics, and the Return to Melanie Klein*, Oxford, R.-U., et Cambridge, É.-U., Blackwell, 1993, p. 17. [Notre traduction.]

5   *Ibid.*

6   Foster, *op. cit.*, p. 273.

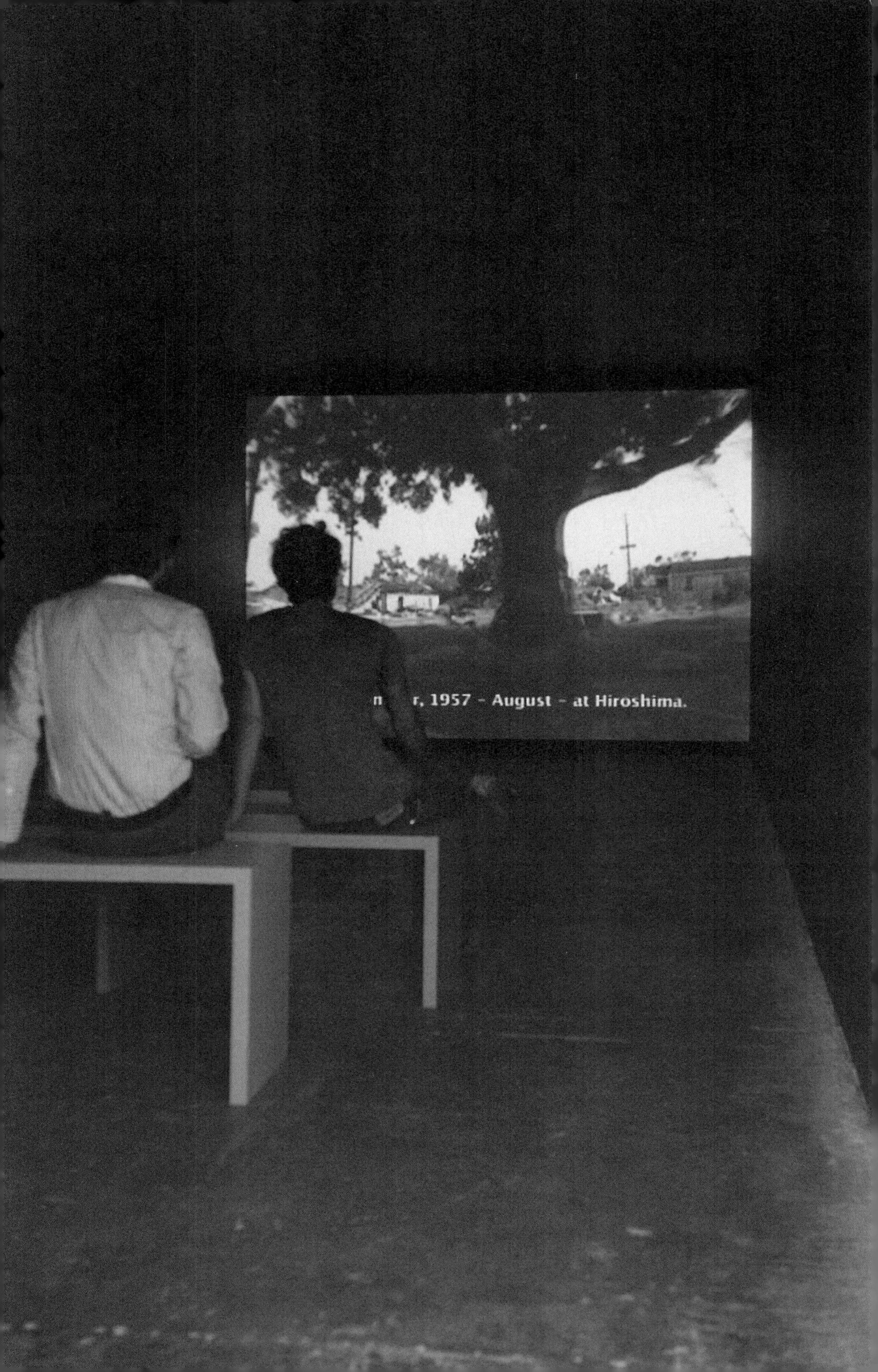
r, 1957 - August - at Hiroshima.

WORKS EXHIBITED / ŒUVRES EXPOSÉES

*an inadequate history
of conceptual art*
1998–1999
Installation
Video, looped, 55 min. /
Vidéo, en boucle, 55 min
Audio, looped, 110 min. /
Audio, en boucle, 110 min
Participants (in alphabetical order, not
playing order / en ordre alphabétique et
non en ordre d'apparition) : Vito Acconci,
Dennis Adams, Mac Adams, Connie Beckley,
Dara Birnbaum, Mel Bochner, Hans Haacke,
Eileen Hickey-Hulme, Mary Kelly,
Joyce Kozloff, Louise Lawler, Les Levine,
Jonas Mekas, Alan McCollum, Howardena
Pindell, Lucio Pozzi, Yvonne Rainer,
Dorothea Rockburne, Al Ruppersberg,
Carolee Schneemann, Lawrence Weiner,
James Welling

*A Film Will Be Shown
Without the Sound*
(Hiroshima mon amour, *1959
Director: Alain Resnais;
Script: Marguerite Duras)*
2006
DVD projection, looped, 90 min. /
Projection DVD, en boucle, 90 min

*After Hiroshima
Mon Amour*
2008
DVD projection, looped; 22 min. /
Projection DVD, en boucle, 22 min
Video and 16 mm b+w /
Vidéo et film 16 mm n+b
Direction / Réalisation : Silvia Kolbowski
Actors / Comédiens : Nuria Carapetian,
Scott Cunningham, Sanjit De Silva,
Tiffany Needham, Roslyn Ruff, Grace
Savage, Sarah Tadloui, Dominik
Tiefenthaler, Anar Vilas, Lana Yoo.
Music and Sound Design / Conception sonore
et musicale : Maxim Kolbowski-Frampton
Video Editing / Montage vidéo :
Maxim Kolbowski-Frampton
Photographic production / Production
photographique : Jeff Barnett-Winsby
Lighting / Éclairage : Jeff Barnett-Winsby
Videography / Vidéographie :
Michael Crane, Erl Kimmich
Sound recording / Enregistrement
sonore : James Wilkins
Sound engineering / Ingénieur
du son : Leslie Lavelanet

*After Hiroshima
Mon Amour*
2008
Inkjet on Dibond / Impression au jet
d'encre sur Dibond
11 panels / 11 panneaux : 40 x 60 cm ;
1 panel / 1 panneau : 40 x 27 cm

All works courtesy the artist / Les œuvres sont présentées
avec l'aimable concours de l'artiste

SILVIA KOLBOWSKI is an artist based in New York. Her scope of address includes the ethics of history, memory, sexuality, and the unconscious. Her 2004 project *Proximity to Power, American Style*, a slide/audio work about the relational aspects of masculine power was published in its entirety by WhiteWalls and University of Chicago Press (2008). In 2007 she exhibited a revised version of her 1999 *an inadequate history of conceptual art* at the Center for Contemporary Art in Warsaw. Her most recent project, a video and photo work entitled *After Hiroshima Mon Amour*, (2008), premiered in September at LAX><ART in Los Angeles, curated by Christopher Bedford. Kolbowski's work has been exhibited internationally, including a 2004 one-person exhibition at the Secession, Vienna, the 2000 Whitney Biennial, The Walker Art Center, and an upcoming installation at The Museum of Modern Art Ljubljana. She is on the advisory board of *October* journal. www.silviakolbowksi.com

SILVIA KOLBOWSKI vit et travaille à New York. Son œuvre traite notamment de l'éthique de l'histoire, de la mémoire, de la sexualité et de l'inconscient. En 2008, *Proximity to Power, American Style*, un projet comprenant une suite de diapositives et un élément audio qui portait sur les aspects relationnels du pouvoir masculin a été publié intégralement par WhiteWalls et University of Chicago Press. Une nouvelle version de *an inadequate history of conceptual art* a été exposée en 2007 au Center for Contemporary Art à Varsovie. Son tout dernier projet intitulé *After Hiroshima Mon Amour* (2008) a été présenté pour la première fois à LAX><ART à Los Angeles par le commissaire Christopher Bedford. Le travail de Kolbowski a fait l'objet d'une importante exposition individuelle à la Secession à Vienne en 2004. Elle a en outre exposé à la Whitney Biennial en 2000, au Walker Art Center et présentera une installation au Musée d'art moderne de Ljubljana. Elle fait partie du conseil consultatif de la revue *October*. www.silviakolbowksi.com

SILVIA KOLBOWSKI
NOTHING AND EVERYTHING
This publication accompanies the exhibition *Silvia Kolbowski: Nothing and Everything*, curated by Michèle Thériault and presented from January 29th to March 7th, 2009 at the Leonard & Bina Ellen Art Gallery, Concordia University. We gratefully acknowledge the financial support of the Canada Council for the Arts.

SILVIA KOLBOWSKI
RIEN ET TOUT
Cette ouvrage accompagne l'exposition *Silvia Kolbowski : Rien et tout*, présentée du 29 janvier au 7 mars 2009 à la Galerie Leonard & Bina Ellen de l'Université Concordia par la commissaire Michèle Thériault. Nous remercions le Conseil des Arts du Canada pour son appui à la réalisation de cet ouvrage.

Publication

Editor / Direction
MICHÈLE THÉRIAULT

Texts / Textes
CHRISTOPHER BEDFORD
ROSALYN DEUTSCHE
SILVIA KOLBOWSKI
MICHÈLE THÉRIAULT

French Translation /
Traduction vers le français
MARIE-JOSÉE ARCAND
COLETTE TOUGAS
MARINE VAN HOOF

Editing / Révision
MICHÈLE THÉRIAULT
SILVIA KOLBOWSKI

Video stills / Images vidéo
SILVIA KOLBOWSKI

Photography / Photographie
KELLIE BARRIE p. 84
HANNES BOECK p. 12–13
TAKAHIRO IMMAMURA p. 11
SILVIA KOLBOWSKI p. 54–55

Photographic Production/
Production photographique
JEFF BARNETT-WINSBY
p. 58–59, 62–63, 64–65, 66–67.

Cover / Couverture
SILVIA KOLBOWSKI

Design / Conception graphique
EMMELYNE PORNILLOS

Printing / Impression
L'EMPREINTE

Binding / Reliure
MULTIRELIURE

*Galerie Leonard & Bina
Ellen Art Gallery*

Direction
MICHÈLE THÉRIAULT

Collections
MÉLANIE RAINVILLE
(Conservatrice Max Stern Curator)

Education and Public Programs /
Éducation et programmes publics
MARINA POLOSA

Exhibition Coordination /
Coordination des expositions
JO-ANNE BALCAEN

Technical direction /
Direction technique
PAUL SMITH

Technicians / Techniciens
ANDREW HARDER
PHILIP KITT

Communications
ANNE-MARIE PROULX

Administration / Secrétariat
ROSETTE ELKESLASSI

Work-Study Students /
Programme Études-travail
ÉLIZABETH BÉLIVEAU
JULIE GAGNON
JASON HENDRICKSON
MARISA HOICKA
ÉTIENNE TREMBLAY-TARDIF
ANTHONY VRAKOTAS

Coop Student / Étudiante coop
STÉPHANIE LAOUN

*Galerie Leonard & Bina
Ellen Art Gallery*

Université Concordia University
1400, boul. de Maisonneuve O., LB 165
Montréal (Québec) Canada H3G 1M8
514-848-2424 # 4750

ellengallery.concordia.ca

978-2-920394-79-7

All rights reserved / Tous droits réservés
Printed in Canada / Imprimé au Canada
© GALERIE LEONARD &
BINA ELLEN ART GALLERY,
CHRISTOPHER BEDFORD,
SILVIA KOLBOWSKI,
MICHÈLE THÉRIAULT

Legal Deposit / Dépôt légal
Bibliothèque nationale et
Archives nationales du Québec
Bibliothèque et Archives
Canada, 2009

Distribution
ABC livres d'art Canada /
ABC Art Books Canada
info@ABCartbookscanada.com